SOCIAL STUDIES
LIBRARY,
WITHDRAWN
SOCIAL STUDIES CENTRE, GEORGE ST
OXFORD. OX1 2RL

D1348928

ST ANTONY'S PAPERS · NUMBER 8

*

# SOUTH ASIAN AFFAIRS

NUMBER ONE

ST ANTONY'S PAPERS

★

NO. 1 SOVIET AFFAIRS: ONE

NO. 2 FAR EASTERN AFFAIRS: ONE

NO. 3 THE ITALIAN LOCAL ELECTIONS 1956

NO. 4 MIDDLE EASTERN AFFAIRS: ONE

NO. 5 THE DECLINE OF THE THIRD REPUBLIC

NO. 6 SOVIET AFFAIRS: TWO

NO. 7 FAR EASTERN AFFAIRS: TWO

Please enter slips under

ST ANTONY'S PAPERS · NUMBER 8

# SOUTH ASIAN AFFAIRS

*Number One*

EDITED BY

RAGHAVAN IYER



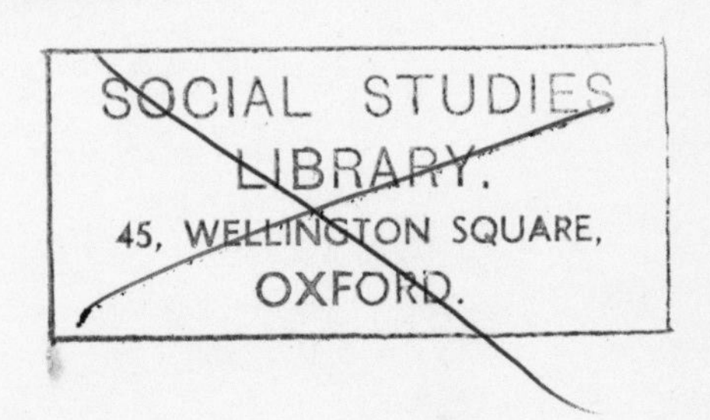


1960
CHATTO & WINDUS
LONDON

PUBLISHED BY
CHATTO AND WINDUS LTD
42 WILLIAM IV STREET
LONDON WC2

*

CLARKE, IRWIN AND CO LTD
TORONTO

PRINTED IN GREAT BRITAIN BY
BUTLER AND TANNER LTD
FROME AND LONDON

# CONTENTS

The main emphasis of the work at St Antony's College, Oxford, since its foundation in 1950 has been in the fields of modern history and international affairs. The College organizes a number of regular Seminars at which are read papers produced by its members in the course of their research or by visiting experts from other institutions. The College further sponsors the delivery of lectures in Oxford by scholars of international reputation in their respective fields.

An appreciable volume of contribution to scholarship is thus being produced under the auspices of St Antony's, and the present series has been started in order to preserve and present a selection of this work. The series is not, however, confined to this material alone and includes contributions from other places.

Three numbers a year are issued and each number is devoted to a particular topic or a particular part of the world.

# UTILITARIANISM AND ALL THAT

## (THE POLITICAL THEORY OF BRITISH IMPERIALISM IN INDIA)

*By Raghavan Iyer*

The political phraseology of the English in India is the same as the political phraseology of our countrymen at home. But it is never to be forgotten that the same words stand for very different things in London and at Calcutta. . . . India cannot have a free government. But she may have the next best thing – a firm and impartial despotism.

MACAULAY[1]

Is a governor in India to consult Puffendorf and Grotius? No. But I will tell you what he is to consult; the laws of nature – not the statutes to be found in those books, nor in any books – but those laws which are to be found in Europe, Africa and Asia, that are to be found amongst all mankind, those principles of equity and humanity implanted in our hearts which have their existence in the feelings of mankind that are capable of judging.

FOX

(i)

IT HAS LONG been an accepted part of the apologetics of modern imperialism to invoke the analogy and the precedent of the Roman Empire. More especially, the comparison has often been made of the role of the British in India and of the Romans in Greece. The Romans and the British, it was plausibly argued, were uniquely able to confer peace and order, law and justice on the peoples they conquered. They were historic instruments of cultural diffusion and political unification and thus rendered an undeniable service even to ancient, self-contained civilizations that were no less advanced than their own. If Lucullus and Dalhousie indulged the appetite for an aggressive, expanding imperialism, there were also those like Cato and Cobden, Scipio and Bright who were averse to an indefinite extension of the area of imperial responsibility. The Romans were better able than the British

[1] References to standard sources are not given in this paper for reasons of space

to assimilate their imperial subjects and to bring them, regardless of race or colour, into the ambit of a common citizenship. The British, on the other hand, were more enlightened than the Romans in their conceptions of the liberty of the subject and the rule of law. Both were convinced that they had far more to give than to receive and tended to conceive of their civilizing mission in messianic terms. In this regard there were rare examples of cultural tolerance and humility among the Romans as well as the British. Cicero, for instance, wrote to his brother Quintus, who was governor of Asia in 60 B.C., that "we are set over a race of men who not only possess the higher culture, but are held to be the source from which it has spread to others". A retired British civil servant of India wrote in 1926 that considerations of racial inequality between rulers and ruled were quite irrelevant. "What race is there should claim superiority to peoples that gave the world a Buddha, an Asoka and an Akbar, religions and philosophies that embrace every religion that has ever existed, an epic literature perhaps unrivalled, and some of the greatest masterpieces in the realm of human art?" And yet, there was a consensus of opinion that the *gravitas* of the true Roman and of the true Briton gave them a title to rule, almost amounting to a divine right, that was lacking in the frivolous and slothful Levantine Greek as well as in the soft and indolent Indian, who was regarded even by Burke as "approaching almost to feminine tenderness". This posture of political condescension could assume absurd proportions and sometimes sink to despicable and dangerous levels But it was in no way comparable to the crude, cruel bigotry of the Spanish Catholic colonists who have been described as "reckless, ruthless, like men intoxicated".

The similarities with the Roman Empire, actual and alleged, cannot do as much as credit to the British Empire as its overriding dissimilarity in one crucial respect – the sense of guilt and the desire for atonement. There was a gnawing doubt from the first that could not be quelled by the passion for fanfare and pride in grandeur that reached their climax under Curzon. As the Oxford classicist, Edwyn Bevan, noticed at the time, the vulgar revelry in vastitude of conquest and even the plea of national self-interest could never satisfy the British rulers as a justification of their Indian empire. As long as the sense of guilt was irrepressible, the self-conscious urge for justification was also inescapable. Outside England, the insistence on moral idealism rather than on material advantage appeared to be either a feeble form of self-deception or a flagrant example of national hypocrisy. How could the sincere moral protestations of English defenders of empire be appreciated by those foreigners who never had a Puritan Revolution and who were never persecuted by their own high principles? What better for men burdened by moral doubts than to disavow considerations of narrow self-interest or shallow grandeur and to invoke the utilitarian creed as an unanswerable justification? Could it not be argued that the British Empire was uniquely useful to the Indian masses, a self-evident fact that was denied by the Indian intelligentsia (those benighted Brahmin "Baboos" and their "crafty" Bania leaders) only because of their innate dishonesty or their neurotic narcissism? To the question, "What right here gave its sanction to might?", surely a ruling race could answer, in all sincerity, in terms of its solemn duty to serve the interests of the ruled and to protect them from their own weaknesses and the designs of ambitious men who exploit the emotions of others for their own ends. Such an answer at any rate comes naturally to those who are sufficiently developed morally to admit, in the first place, that there is a question to be answered.

Today, more than ever before, the utilitarian plea comes in handy as an *ex post facto* justification. It is now fortunately unfashionable to talk openly of the civilizing mission of the white races, of the sacred responsibilities of self-appointed, Platonic guardians or even the austere and tedious tasks of trusteeship assumed as a result of the accidents of history if not as an act of Providence. In the early phase of the acquirement of power, its instrumental value is stressed. As power becomes concentrated in a settled ruling class and exercised through recognized institutions and procedures, it tends to become a self-justifying phenomenon. The fact that it is such a vital element in the pursuit of other and even laudable goals tends to transform its very nature. When power is lost, or when it is shed, it cannot be retrospectively justified as an autonomous value which is somehow identified with all other values that are deemed worthwhile. It must be seen entirely as an instrumental value that is judged solely by its fruits. The temptation is strong to explain away, or to conceal, or to deny, past tendencies to pursue it beyond all other values. This temptation has been splendidly resisted by Professor Thornton in his *The Imperial Idea and its Enemies*. Further, it can clearly be shown, as has been brilliantly done by Professor Stokes in his *English Utilitarians and India*, that utilitarianism is not just a convenient device of imperialist self-defence on meeting its end. It was actually the deliberate policy of a gifted and eccentric ruling class in those formative years before the Crown took over from the Company full responsibility for the government of the Indian subcontinent. It can, therefore, be all the more easily fitted into an elegant Whig-Imperialist model often used by hacks to celebrate, not merely justify, the record of British rule in Asia. The British not only transmitted to an alien, Asiatic people the spirit of the European Renaissance and of the Reformation and the Enlightenment. They not only extended an aristocratic Establishment from an island to a global empire. They also exported the Age of Reform from Liberal England, the virtues of public probity and State philanthropy, and the magic carpet of collectivism in harmony with private enterprise, to an under-developed continent in its pre-industrial state of nature. The Government of India was regarded at times as "not only a government but the chief landlord", as "an improving proprietor on an enormous scale". British rule had to "play the part of universal provider and special providence". To cap it all, the British were not only responsible for "the introduction in the midst of Brahmins of European views of the universe". They also gave away the secret weapons of petitioning authority and even of engineering a relatively bloodless revolution. Just as voters worked for the voteless, Christians for the emancipation of the Jews, masters for the abolition of slavery and Protestants for the emancipation of the Catholics, so the British helped to free their subjects from their political slavery. All this special pleading is perfectly understandable and makes enough sense of the facts to become the basis of popular political mythology today. If nationalists, on the other side, need to re-write history along Promethean lines of continuous, determined revolt against absolute tyranny, if they need to meet every plea of expediency with the sovereign talisman of the natural rights of all men under the universal sway of natural law, imperialist writers on their side require the holy name of Utility to provide a further *raison d'être* for Raison d'Etat. And so the debate goes on, from the Indian Empire of yesterday to the Central African Federation of our own day.

(ii)

The appeal from imperialism to utilitarianism has interesting consequences not only for appreciating Indo-British relations and modern imperial history, but also for a study of liberal political theory and the two faces of utilitarianism. Utilitarian considerations are not merely the basis of representative democracy and liberal capitalism. They can also be equally employed to justify authoritarian régimes and enlightened, benevolent despotism. Interference with the negative liberties of others is not only justifiable (rightly or wrongly) in terms of idealistic metaphysics and occult references to higher selves and real wills. It could also be defended in terms of the "real" and long-term interests of others that may be unknown to them. Negative liberty itself, the area within which a man can do what he wants, may equally be justified by the utilitarian argument that a man needs the licence to do what he wants as by a purer moral plea that a man's power of choice is somehow sacred and, therefore, inalienable. Once, however, the utilitarian element enters into the notion of liberty, the danger of justifiable coercion arises in a subtle manner through the argument that a man may be trained how to choose and how to know what his needs and all his wants are. More generally and more plausibly an imperialist could claim that he can protect the negative liberties of his subjects better than they could do by themselves or through representatives of their own race and nationality. It is not, therefore, surprising that the nationalist has to retaliate against a theory of authoritarian utilitarianism by producing a theory of transferred natural rights, i.e. by basing the sanctity of individual personality on its supposed connection with national status.

The abuse of notions of positive liberty, general will and higher selves is not peculiar to them. The fact that it is more common is only because these notions have a wider political currency and a greater moral force. Seminal political concepts are interdependent and interdefinable. We can only anathematize the most vulnerable concepts by taking a partial and incomplete view of political theory itself. Such a course is open to the critic but not to the creator of political systems, although the critic can point to the special and dispensable presuppositions that the great system-builders assume without question to be absolute. Utilitarianism, like every original and powerful political doctrine, can be and has been invoked on behalf of authority as well as freedom, as a theory of government as well as a theory of society. It not merely recognized each man's right to seek his own happiness but also championed the duty of the state to produce, by deliberate and systematic interference, a harmony of interests. It incorporated the element of benevolence stressed by Hutcheson as well as the element of coercion and even of ruthlessness by means of which Hobbes pushed utilitarian ideas to totalitarian extremes. The young Bentham was an advocate of enlightened despotism and never became a whole-hearted democrat. The elder Mill believed that happiness and not liberty was the end of government. He formulated in its extreme form the absurdly extravagant doctrine of "Oriental despotism" which provided an alibi for the translation of British utilitarianism into the theory and policy of imperialism in India. His son's passionate concern for liberty led him to assert that it was impossible for one people to govern another. At the same time the influence of his father's *History of India* made him deny the applicability of his theories of liberty and of representative government to the conditions prevalent in Eastern dependencies. Although he felt himself at a great distance from his father's "tone of thought and feeling", he found that they were "almost always in strong agreement on the political questions of the day". He also found many points of sympathy between him and Austin, who "never ceased to be a utilitarian" and thought that "there was more practical good government under the Prussian monarchy than under the English representative government".

The authoritarian element in British utilitarianism easily lent itself to serve imperialist ends as well as imperialist theories of self-justification. Imperialist experience in its turn further weakened and sometimes destroyed the feeling for the liberal element in utilitarianism. To Milner, both the British Constitution and the party system were "antiquated and bad" as they undermined the effectiveness of positive Government. To Fitzjames Stephen, who was more Hobbesian than Bentham or Austin, John Stuart Mill had perverted the pure doctrine of his father by yoking it to popular liberalism. The task of government was to impose the ideal of happiness of a gifted ruling class upon a passive majority that had to be saved from all anarchic tendencies. But such ideas, like the earlier nabobs and the latter-day sahibs who returned to England, were strangers in the land of their birth. Apart from the liberal heritage of the past, the rising power of the middle classes was hostile in an era of expanding trade to autocratic and bureaucratic government. Liberty at home could thus coexist with despotism abroad. The expansion of England required a compromise between conflicting principles that the country could well afford. Disraeli's formula, *Imperium et Libertas*, left it open whether empire or liberty was to be the ruling principle and the dominant theme in English life, although Disraeli preferred the former, for it was "as selfish as patriotism". Even Gladstone, who could become ecstatic about liberty, thought that "the sentiment of empire may be called innate in every Briton. If there are exceptions, they are like those of men born blind or lame among us. It is part of our patrimony: born with our birth, dying only with our death; incorporating itself in the first elements of our knowledge, and interwoven with all our habits of mental action upon public affairs." [2]

It is possible to argue that if we are justified in condemning Rousseau by Robespierre, Hegel by Hitler and Marx by Stalin, we are also entitled to judge Bentham by Bentinck, Burke by Curzon and the two Mills by those who invoked the notion of Oriental despotism to oppose every demand for political progress in India. The search for scapegoats whose crucifixion can atone for monstrous systems of error and evil is itself based, however, on an unduly rationalistic faith in the influence of theory and on an absurdly simple view of both individual and national character. Herder may have good reason to assert that a history of opinions would really be the key to the history of deeds. It is, however, one thing to stress the impact of ideas and opinions on policies and actions. It is quite another matter to single out certain thinkers or theories or concepts as responsible for what they could neither have visualized nor intended in all its implications. The historian of ideas is, as Meinecke so clearly saw, "no mere shadow-play or sequence of grey theories; on the contrary, it is the life-blood of events, absorbed into the life-blood of those men who are called upon to express the essential element of their epoch". In pleading against the tyrannical and tragic consequences of isms and systems, we may foist too easily the entire burden of blame upon those very thinkers whose theories were most vulnerable to distortion as well as exploitation. Political theories may be rejections as well as rationalizations of features of national tradition. Political thinkers may revolt against prevalent social conditions and political forms and practices either because of nostalgia or utopianism, anarchistic discontent or optimism, or because they cannot comprehend the social forces of their time. They are as much the product of their national tradition and temperament as those who use and abuse their theories in later epochs, or while

[2] "England's Mission", *The Nineteenth Century*, September 1878

they are still alive. The subtle connection between ideas and acts, theories and policies as well as between ideas and excuses, theories and slogans can be reduced to a stark simplicity if we take a monistic view of human motive and adopt a harsh certainty with regard to human nature, if we are too behaviouristic and too deterministic in our approach. The ideas as well as the intentions behind any system of power should not, however, be regarded as good or evil *per se*. We can never be clear or certain enough to draw up an indictment (or a panegyric) against a whole people, or against a ruling class.

The over-estimation of theory as well as the over-simplification of ideas and intentions must especially be safeguarded against in the case of the British who have ever been empiricists *par excellence*. It is not merely that inconsistency of character and absence of definite aim are most notable Anglo-Saxon qualities, as Cromer thought. It is not so much that the Englishman has no general ideas, as Dilke asserted. Nor is it just that the English governing class has more highly developed than any other a sense of the possible and has an almost prophetic knowledge of when it is necessary to retreat. The late André Siegfried came closest to the heart of the matter when he said[3] that the Englishman acts like an old-time sailor who manœuvres in an unstable environment and who believes that nature does not allow man to meet every contingency with ready-made, tidy solutions. Further, the Protestant Englishman, unlike the Catholic Frenchman, assumes personal responsibility for his actions and feels the need for atonement rather than for absolution, because it is with his own conscience and sense of duty that he must settle his affairs. For this reason, perhaps, the Englishman sometimes became almost insensitive to the feelings of others and behaved imperially like a Victorian nanny. J. S. Mill attributes his father's deficiency in tenderness to his being English. Henri Bourassa, the French-Canadian nationalist, complained that in spite of his remarkable faculties for government, and the general humanity of his proceedings, the Anglo-Saxon did not know how to gain the confidence, much less the affection, of the peoples that he dominated. It is, however, easy to create an Aunt Sally out of English national character. It is also absurd to read too much into English history and to assert that the Englishman is anti-revolutionary because he is too dull to take in a great idea and too selfish to apply it to any interest save his own. It may well be, as a contemporary English socialist has

[3] *The Character of Peoples*, chapter 4

argued, that "the picture given by British political theorists of 'man the political animal' belies at every point the British political animal. The former is a cool and calculating hedonist, bound by no ties which self-interest cannot justify; the latter is a sentimentalist, content to accept ancestral institutions and modify them to existing circumstances according to the mysterious canons of fair play." It is certainly true that the Englishman, while willing to display abroad his talent for compromise and conciliation to a lesser extent than at home, was tempted to experiment in the colonies with theories that were distrusted in practice in his own country. But even here it is possible to argue that the actual policies were of less importance in some cases than the particular men whom we praise or blame for implementing them in their own peculiar way.

(iii)

The British empire in India was, of course, *sui generis*. It still seems incredible that a handful of Englishman could rule an alien and ancient civilization of many millions over a vast and varied subcontinent for over a century with a mixture of motives and methods, policies and principles that baffles analysis and defies explanation. Mill said in his *Autobiography* that no government had, on the whole, given so much proof, to the extent of its lights, of good intention towards its subjects. And yet, Munro could write as early as 1818 to Hastings: "Foreign conquerors have treated the natives with violence, and often with great cruelty, but none has treated them with so much scorn as we." Macaulay proclaimed in 1833 that the Indian Empire, "the strangest of all political anomalies", resembled no other in history and formed by itself a separate class of political phenomena so that its growth and decay were regulated by unknown laws. It could certainly be contended that the "unnatural connection" between England and India was the result of some abnormality in India rather than in England. The brightest jewel in the Crown was at no time nearly as important to England as the politics of the nearby European states. England, which had valiantly resisted Spanish imperialism in the 16th century, French imperialism in the 19th century and German imperialism in the 20th century, could never become deeply agitated about its own imperialism in India. Within India itself, the spiritual and cultural exclusiveness of the Hindu and the social and intellectual aloofness of the English fostered a gulf between rulers and ruled that seemed to be unbridgeable and only to grow rather than to narrow with the passage of time. The sense of alienation was at all times overpowering and total in its nature except for a fortunate few. Most of them could cross the cultural barrier only by losing their own roots, by tearing themselves away from the tyranny of caste on either side. Despite the petty prejudices of men, the historical forces released by the Indo-British connection were of enormous magnitude and enduring significance. India unwillingly facilitated the Industrial Revolution in England and England unwittingly stimulated the Indian Renaissance. The inevitable clash and involuntary contact between races and between cultures were almost cosmic in their effects, for Asia and Europe never met so fruitfully since the ephemeral expedition to India of Alexander of Macedon. The results of the British encounter with India may yet prove to be more far-reaching and even deeper than the consequences of the Roman Empire.

The mid-Victorian Radicals in England were deeply concerned about the consequences of the empire for their own country as well as for the helpless colonies, and protested against the prevalent mood of casual complacency. Cobden could see no advantage either to the natives or to their foreign masters in this vast Indian possession and was aware that "a feeling of alienation was constantly increasing with both the natives and the English". Furthermore, if a Board of Works could not give a common sewer for London, was it likely to cover India with canals for irrigation? If Catholic and Protestant could not live together peacefully in Belfast, were the British the people to teach Christian charity to the Hindus? The British had adopted in India "the principle of a military despotism" and such an undertaking could only be "a calamity and a curse to the people of England". Bright was bothered about the cost of governing India and the meagre sums spent upon its people compared to the "monstrous" salaries paid to British officials. The edifice reared was too vast for management and there was no man competent to govern the whole of India. If India were to be governed for the good of England, the good of England must come through the channels of the good of India, and India must become rich in order that England may become rich. If India was to be governed and not to be abandoned, "calumny" against Indians must cease. They had the highest claims on their rulers who must recognize that there was a judgment for nations as for individuals. There was a higher and holier glory than military conquest and that could come through conferring solid and lasting benefits upon the Indian people. The system of government had to be changed, for "what would be thought if the whole of Europe was under one governor, who knew only the language of the Feejee Islands"? If they retained the "fatal gift of empire" without the ability to govern it, finally India would be avenged. If, on the other hand, they were willing to prepare for the time when India will have to take up her own government, they would be "endeavouring to make amends for the original crime upon which much of our power in India is founded, and for the many mistakes which have been made by men whose intentions have been good". The Radicals were voices in the wilderness. Their influence was not immediate or obvious, their ideas were never consciously or fully carried out. Yet they provided one element in British imperialism in India that was muted, but never wholly discarded. The concept of atonement lingered till the empire came to its end, under the auspices of Attlee.

Other elements were, however, more to the fore most of the time. There was the noble Roman element, the desire to maintain the rule of law and to cherish the *pax Britannica*, the sheer concern for good government in the most earthy sense but on a grand scale. This was well expressed by the Earl of Mayo in his address at Ajmere in 1869 to the princes and chiefs of Rajputana. He then pleaded "that justice and order shall prevail, that every man's property shall be secure, that the traveller shall come and go in safety, that the cultivator shall enjoy the fruits of his labours, and the trader the produce of his commerce: that you shall make roads, and undertake the construction of those works or irrigation which will improve the condition of the people and swell the revenues of your states: that you shall encourage education and provide for the relief of the sick". Then there was the exclusive, Semitic element, the calm belief that the English were the elect, divinely appointed to bear the white man's burden for the benefit of those beyond the pale. This was proclaimed most clearly by Disraeli, easily combined with the prevailing notions of political Darwinism, and later on popularized by Kipling. "Progress and reaction," declared Disraeli, "are but words . . . all is race." In *Coningsby* he said that "Toryism indeed is but copied from the mighty prototype which has fashioned Europe". In *Lord George Bentinck* he observed that the Jews are the trustees of tradition, "a living and the most striking evidence of the falsity of that pernicious doctrine of modern times, the natural equality of man". He was profoundly convinced of the inherent superiority of English, as of Jewish, blood, and the consequent righteousness of making a Promised Land of the territory of others. His conception of the British Empire had a magical glow for those who were within the charmed circle. If England was to maintain her empire, she must come to believe in her uniqueness so completely that other peoples – at any rate in her dependent territories – would come to believe it as well. For him, colonies possessed intrinsic and not merely instrumental value. Even in 1866, when Chancellor of the Exchequer, he had written that "Power and influence we should exercise in Asia; consequently in Eastern Europe, consequently also in Western Europe". The empire needed its loyal believers and champions. The climax of emotion came when Queen Victoria was proclaimed Empress of India in 1877. Then there was the aggressive Prussian element, the pride in military power, the deification of discipline, the requirement of docility in the ruled, the justification of brutality and violence to overthrow militant opposition to the régime. This element was rather rare but it did exist, especially at intermediate levels of the hierarchy. It was partially expressed by Michael O'Dwyer, Governor of the Punjab, who defended General Dyer's action at Amritsar, and who condemned Montagu for his "sentimental, futile and humiliating policy". He had no use for the Congress which created disaffection among the simple and credulous masses and he was in favour of crushing "the insidious campaign of Peaceful Rebellion". He quoted with approval Churchill's statement in 1930 that "Gandhism and all it stands for will sooner or later have to be grappled with and finally crushed. It is of no use trying to satisfy a tiger with scraps of cat's meat." He wanted a policy of "firmness" rather than of "vague idealism" and felt that the Parliament must be "of more robust spirit" and not "the slave of catchwords and slogans" which would lead it to throw away "our great Indian Empire, the greatest achievement of the British race".

British imperialism in India was thus compounded of diverse and even contradictory elements, the chief of which were the Roman (or Asokan or Buddhist) element of peace under law; the Semitic (or Brahmin) element of racial exclusiveness and destiny; the Prussian (or Moghul or Kautilyan) element of militancy and firmness; and the nonconformist Radical (or Christian or Hindu) element of atonement and penance and expiation. These elements were embodied in the principles of government, the men who were selected to carry the burden of administration and the institutional structure of the imperial system. The principles reflected the aims and needs of a just but alien, a firm but not conscienceless, despotism. The governing class was a proud and exclusive caste, conscious of its political and military power, anxious to preserve the peace and to maintain the rule of law, occasionally troubled by moral qualms or mental doubts. The system consisted of a centralized judiciary and police force, a narrowly based and well-bred civil service, a powerful state with a competent intelligence wing and a disciplined army, and a slow extension of minimal opportunities for the expression of public grievances and moderate opposition to the government. It is important to keep some sort of balance between the relative roles of the personalities who constituted the ruling class, the theories that influenced their policies, and the system which was set up and acquired in time a distinctive shape and decisive significance.

Curzon may have been right in stating that "Government goes by personality". But when he pleaded in his farewell speech to the Byculla Club that "one-man supervision is the very best form of government, presuming the man to be competent", and that the only alternative was "a most mechanical and lifeless" bureaucracy, he was, in fact, voicing a particular theory of centralized, personal rule that others disliked. A reaction was bound to set in. After all, even the doctrines of German idealism before 1800 acquired political significance only in the Prussian bureaucracy. The servants of the crown embraced "seditious ideas" and invoked the liberal principles of Kant to undermine the soulless rigour and intolerant oppressiveness of Frederick's rulership. Individual freedom to think, the right to dissent, became "the gateway to professional happiness, to self-disciplined discretionary action . . . and to the replacement of erratic dynastic autocracy by a more magnanimous and more efficient form of despotic government, by humanized bureaucratic absolutism, 'which will find it advantageous to itself to treat man, who thenceforth is more than a machine, in accord with his dignity.' "[4] Many apologists for the British Empire would prefer to argue that bad theories were applied by good administrators than *vice versa*. They would even like to think that the theories as well as the men who applied (or modified or ignored) them were good rather than bad, taking everything into account. Mr Philip Woodruffe has invoked the Christian maxim that men should be judged by their best rather than by their worst and presumably also rejects the apparently

[4] Hans Rosenberg, *Bureaucracy, Democracy and Autocracy*, 1958, p. 189

Semitic belief that theories should be judged by their worst rather than by their best applications. It would indeed be a counsel of perfection to demand that we must always judge all men and all theories after taking their best as well as their worst acts and applications into full consideration. But, surely, we must at least maintain a level of consistency and fairness that are required both by true intellectual standards and by all religious teaching. If we wish to judge men by their best, we must do so with nationalists as well as with imperialists and *vice versa*, which the followers of no religion find easy to do. If we wish to judge theories by their worst formulations and results, we must do so with those which appeal to as us well as with those which annoy us from the start, which intellectuals of all types find easier to attempt than to achieve.

There is clearly something to be said for an examination of the theories involved in British government in India. They are at least less difficult to detect than the complex motives that governed the conduct of the varied men who made up an entire ruling class. If nothing else is gained, we can at any rate try to prevent the enthroning of a particular theory or school of thinkers as the chief determinant over a century of foreign rule. In the twenties Huxley commented on the haphazard oscillation between contrary theories that was dictated by the changing circumstances of British rule in India.

> Old and new strangely coexist, and India is ruled in accordance with two completely incompatible theories of government: that of Akbar, shall we say, and that of Woodrow Wilson. On Monday the watchword of the executive is "Reform and responsible self-government"; like Oliver Twist the Indians immediately ask for more: their demands become increasingly insistent, and the Government nervously decides to be firm. On Tuesday some General Dyer rivals the exploits of the Moghuls; repressive legislation is passed, the gaols are crowded. On Wednesday the Government is seized with qualms. Remembering what Mr Gladstone said in 1882 and why the Great War was fought, it makes a "generous gesture". The response is so unenthusiastic that it becomes necessary on Thursday to suspend the Habeas Corpus Act and imprison several thousand suspects without a trial. By the end of the week everybody, including the Government itself, is feeling rather muddled.[5]

[5] *Jesting Pilate*

The state of muddle was even more complicated over the entire period of British rule in India. There were, at least, four distinct strands – the Burkean doctrine of imperial trusteeship, the utilitarian theory of state activity that was propounded mainly by Bentham but also by the two Mills, the Platonic conception of a ruling elite that would act as wise guardians, and the Evangelical zeal to spread the gospel so as to elevate the character and save the souls of even perversely unwilling people. Each of these strands had several aspects and assumed a variety of forms, with differing degrees of theoretical purity and practical debasement. The pure Burkean doctrine was distorted, especially at times of stress, by the Prussian element in imperialism so that the solemn trustees could become overbearing and even oppressive. They were sometimes translated into petty tyrants of whom Burke would never have approved. The Benthamite doctrine could degenerate into Hobbesian coercion and concentration of power, but it was also sublimated by the Roman element in British imperialism into a theory of legal unification and state philanthropy. The Platonic doctrine was sometimes enhanced by a Whig belief in liberalism and in progress, but it was also pathetically perverted to the point of caricature by the Semitic element in British imperialism which gave the concept of the chosen race. The Evangelical doctrine gave rise to many religious fears and resentments among the Indian people, but it was fortunately counterbalanced by the nonconformist Radical element in British imperialism, by the Christian notion of atonement which required that a believer should not neglect his own sins while saving the souls of brethren beyond the pale. The Burkean doctrine could be used to support the view that the British had greatness thrust upon them. The Benthamite doctrine could show that Britain could become great by her activities abroad. The Platonic doctrine could be taken to mean that the British were born great, with an innate right to rule over others. The Evangelical doctrine could be used to assert that the greatness to be sought and secured was not of this world and lay far in the future, as a reward for present efforts to extend the influence on earth of the divine word and the divine will. The trustees had to take "Oriental stagnation" for granted and to display a profound distrust of the new Indian intelligentsia, from whom the varied peasantry and their ancestral traditions had to be protected. The utilitarians were saved from disturbing doubts about their own policies by the bogey of "Oriental despotism" and by their belief in the need for social reform and popular education. The guardians had to remind themselves continually about "Oriental backwardness" and the inferiority of the Indian ruling class which was nearing its natural demise, leaving the rest in the position of Peter Pan. The Peter Pan theory of India, as J. A. Spender called it, was compounded of two separate ideas – the East is unchanging and Orientals are like children. The evangelicals took for granted that "Oriental superstition and vice" could not be met by anything in Indian religious tradition as they were directly and causally connected. A policy of non-interference or of toleration of Indian religions was solely a matter of temporary expediency and even an invitation to divine vengeance, which came in the form of the Mutiny. Besides the four chief strands of theory, there were no doubt minor elements derived from Aristotle, Locke, Austin, T. H. Green, Spencer and Buckle and several others. But the influence of these was intermittent and limited in scope and in their applicability to the central problem of imperial government in India. The Burkean, Benthamite, Platonic and Evangelical doctrines were useful for imperial administration as well as apologetics. They could be made the basis of a theory of government, a theory of society and a theory of history which were adaptable to the needs of a highly centralized system of benevolent and durable despotism over an alien, vast and diverse population in a distant subcontinent.

(iv)

"All empire is power in trust," said Dryden in *Absalom and Achitophel.* Nowhere has this concept been so clearly stated as in the speeches of Burke. In his celebrated oration on Fox's India Bill in 1783, Burke asserted that government is "in the strictest sense a trust". All political power set over men and all privileges claimed against the natural equality of mankind ought to be some way or other exercised ultimately for their benefit. Further, "it is of the very essence of every trust to be rendered accountable, and even totally to cease, when it substantially varies from the purposes for which alone it could have a lawful existence". Trustees had "no right to make a market" of their duties. If a trust held derivatively is abused, "the contract is broken" and the holders of the trust originally re-enter into all all their rights, i.e. into the exercise of all their duties. Parliament had no sort of "epicurean excuse to stand aloof". British governors ought to "govern on

British principles, not by British forms", said Burke five years later, calling for a spirit of equity, justice, protection and "lenity" and attacking the notion of "geographical morality". At the same time he pleaded against forcing on others "the narrow circle of our ideas" regarding custom and usage. He insisted that Oriental governments know nothing of arbitrary power even if the British have better institutions for the preservation of the rights of men than any other country in the world. In Asia as in Europe "the same law of nations prevails", the same political principles and maxims are "continually resorted to" and "strenuously maintained". Burke took pains to examine "the constitution of Oriental governments" and came to the view that "Asia is enlightened in that respect as well as Europe". No one in modern Europe has more stoutly spurned the facile aspersion of "Oriental despotism". He displayed an imagination and a tolerance lacking in liberals like Macaulay. Burke was more anxious to reform the English trustees in India than their numerous subjects with their ancient beliefs and diverse customs, "a people for ages civilized and cultivated; cultivated by all the arts of polished life, while we were yet in the woods". He was against every form of "social engineering" or "political geometry" which sprang from the Jacobin simplification of man. He believed that circumstances give to every political principle "its distinguishing colour and discriminating effect". But Burke had a notion of government and of trusteeship which required that human wants should be provided for by human wisdom, even against individual as well as collective inclinations. He could go as far as to say that "the restraints on men, as well as their liberties, are to be reckoned among their rights". There was even a proprietary as well as a contractual element in Burke's notion of government; the rights of government were almost a form of private ownership. "State" and "Estate" were almost identical so that public and private affairs could not be sharply differentiated. It is not surprising that Burke's social philosophy and his notion of history were behind the outlook of men like Munro, Malcolm, Metcalfe and Elphinstone. The conception of benevolent landlordism combined a Benthamite theory of government with a Burkean view of society. Social conservatism was wedded for a time to a liberal spirit of reform.

The Burkean doctrine of trusteeship was common to conservatives and to liberals, although their differences as to the period of transition and the policies to be followed were serious enough not to be wholly obscured by the illusion of permanency that they both began to share. Even the radicals were influenced by the doctrine of trusteeship, although they had their fears about its feasibility. The natives, said Bright, were like sheep without a shepherd. The doctrine remained, however, essentially conservative, for it usually went with a reverence for the past, a distrust of theory, an organic conception of society, a feeling for constitutional continuity, a stress upon loyalty and *esprit de corps*, a concern with duties rather than with rights, a belief in the complexity of human nature and in the secondary importance of politics, a love of fox-hunting ("the wisest religion", as Quintin Hogg called it), the dream of a *civitas dei* distinct from the political system, the acceptance of a religious basis for civil society and the view that all universal ideas must be modified in terms of common sense and expediency so as to allow for what Disraeli called "the necessities of nations". Burke wanted the trustees to be "faithful watchmen" over the rights and privileges of the people, while he had no use for what Coleridge later on condemned as the "talismanic influence" of legislation. Burke is really not the philosopher of British conservatism alone, but of British political life from Right to Left, especially when projected abroad. Gladstone, Ramsay MacDonald and Lansbury all took for granted the deep organic conservatism of British social life. Despite the language of interest and reason and the preaching of utilitarianism, the imperial ruling class, with its continuity of tradition and fluidity of membership, cherished in practice the fragile bonds of collective sentiment and conscience and evolved their own handy notions of what constituted "the rules of the game" and "fair play".

The doctrine of trusteeship was taken seriously even to the extent that in practice it meant an unwillingness to delegate responsibility and to trust the natives to do anything for themselves. The trustees assumed that they alone loved and knew the *real* India and what began as an underestimation of the new Indian intelligentsia became in time a fierce phobia. References were made to the "Oriental spider" and the "cold, calculated lie" of those who wilfully and maliciously "misled" the masses by wild tirades and millennial intimations. Even the saintly Gandhi was most cheaply vilified as the "Dangerous Feminine Man". Similarly, the trustees resented "the petty fanaticism of the meddlesome prigs", of their critics at home. The "calumny of the natives", as Bright called it, led in time to the slander of compatriots who refused to conform. The Baboos whom the Sahibs abominated did not realize that the Sahibs were not loved everywhere in England. The doctrine of trusteeship was tragically perverted by a racialism that was not essential to it together with a messianic element that was imported into it. There was a mandate towards the natives as well as a mandate of responsibility to the civilized world. Imperialism was regarded as a wider, grander concept than nationalism. Representative government had to be sacrificed to responsible government. On the other hand, the transitional element in the doctrine of trusteeship could also not be completely forgotten. Mill had spoken of the need to facilitate the transition of the subject people to a higher state of improvement. When he was Lieutenant-Governor, Lyall wrote: "One thing is sure; the natives all discuss our rule as a transitory state." This was not welcome to the trustees. Earlier, Lord Lytton had written that "we have had to choose between prohibiting them (i.e. the natives) and cheating them, and we have chosen the least straightforward course". Later on, he said of Lord Ripon's policy, "Does it not mean, nay, ought it not to be taken as meaning that we, the English Government in India, feel ourselves in a false position from which we wish to extricate ourselves as quickly as possible?" No one appreciated and accepted the logic of the theory of trusteeship as fully as Sir Henry Cotton or Lionel Curtis early in this century. Lytton had already pointed to the mistake of the earlier trustees that they could "hold India securely by what they call good government". Maine had showed that the trustees could not help the dissolving force that Western civilization had brought on traditional Indian society; they could not supply social cohesion. In the late twenties J. A. Spender attacked the other assumption of the trustees, that they could appeal to the peasants over the heads of the politicians or even that they understood their needs and grievances better than men like Gandhi.

Was the doctrine of trusteeship inherently erroneous and not merely vulnerable? Was it merely a theory trotted out to justify what Cobden called "a gigantic system of outdoor relief for the aristocracy"? Was it a species of cant, a kind of moral slang? Was Hobson's charge of hypocrisy against "phrase-mongering" imperialists a denial of the validity of the doctrine of trusteeship in theory as well as in practice? Could it not be argued that every trustee abused his powers and that the entire theory was an ideal fiction? The fact remains that we cannot dispense with ideal fictions or pleasing emotions or moral slogans in politics. The doctrine of trusteeship provided what proved to be in practice more a private moral code than a generally accepted theory of government. It is possible to doubt the wisdom of imperial conquest and yet to accept the moral problem faced by colonial rule as requiring some sort of practicable solution. There was in Burke a Platonic idealism regarding what governments as well as individuals could achieve. The chief merit of the old feudal system was that "it made power gentle and obedience liberal". He also appealed to Roman political practice based on the belief in private honour as the great foundation of public trust so that private and public virtues were harmoniously combined rather than mutually destructive. If the Burkean doctrine appeared later on to be a formula borrowed from the missionary by the politician to cover up the naked fact of domination, this was because of the sense of alienation, the absence of mutual sympathy between rulers and ruled against which the theory of trusteeship must gradually break down even while bringing inspiration to the finest spirits among the possessors of a monopoly of political power. If they could not regard themselves as the trustees of the interests and fortunes of many millions, they could at least gain acceptance by their everyday acts as just conciliators in local disputes between men of different sects and castes and social groups.

## (v)

It was perhaps the lofty remoteness of the doctrine of trusteeship that made the Benthamite doctrine of utilitarianism so convenient both as a form of justification and as a practical basis of imperial rule. It is indeed ironical that a rather provincial creed should have achieved world-wide influence. Cromer had argued that if good use was made of imperial power, the British need not fear that they would be overtaken by the Nemesis which attended Roman misrule. It could, in fact, be contended that if the Roman Empire spread Christianity, the British Empire disseminated the creed of Utilitarianism. It resulted in the *malaise religieux* in India even if it did not, as many expected, sweep away the panorama of classic Hindu "paganism". The Utilitarian creed, in general, despite its wide sway, did not excite much enthusiasm except among the utilitarians themselves, who constituted a sort of Whig oligarchy, with a few men of outstanding competence and a large quantity of self-satisfied, mediocre imitators. They rejected all transcendental talk of natural law and cosmic purpose and became conscious of the immediate possibilities of political power. They were chiefly the heirs of Humean scepticism, Hobbesian realism and the "Theological Utilitarianism" of Cumberland and Paley, but they were not aware of this lineage so much as the living leadership of Bentham, "the father of English innovation", "the great subversive". He swept away Burke's own abstractions, denounced complication as "the nursery of fraud" and set himself up as a simplifier. His belief in single judges, his deprecation of juries, his eulogy of summary modes of procedure, his contempt for the doctrine of separation of powers, his enormous faith in the potentialities of executive power and his conception of legislation as a panacea were all characteristic of his thought. For security against breach of trust, the sole apt remedy was, in his view, not impotence but constant responsibility, "substantial, punitional and dislocational". His concern was with authority, not liberty, individual or national. He was strenuously opposed to the notion of natural rights, "nonsense upon stilts". A Declaration of Rights, which to Burke was the "Digest of Anarchy", was to Bentham an evil, "the *ne plus ultra* of metaphysics". Despite the arguments he supplied the Radicals, he came to the view that the colonies could not be emancipated. They were possible laboratories for social and political experiment. Even at the end of his life he said that Mill would be the living executive and he would be the dead legislative of British India. Mill was able to exercise a more direct influence as he was, in the language of the Radicals, a "retainer from the other side", a "demagogue" at home and a despot abroad. In his evidence of 1832 before the Parliamentary Committee, he put forth his notion of a Government of India, supreme over all courts and persons, with absolute authority equal to that of the British Parliament and with a single legislative council of experts. It did not matter so much *who* governed as long as the business of government was discharged efficiently and cheaply. If the people were properly protected, their character would be elevated effortlessly. His son, J. S. Mill, also held a lofty view of the need for active supervision and control from London as there was no practical alternative to a pure and enlightened, benevolent despotism. But he never denied the abstract right of India to self-governing institutions, and in this sense alone it could be said that he civilized Utilitarianism.

Two years after Bentinck became Governor-General, Bentham wrote to Bentinck that he felt "as if the golden age of British India were lying before me". Bentinck declared that the first and primary object of his heart was the benefit of the Hindus and that a new morality and a new conception of the will of God would be useful in improving their future condition. "I write and feel as a legislator for the Hindus, and as I believe many enlightened Hindus think and feel." The same "enlightened principles" could promote in India as in England the general prosperity and also exalt the character of the British. They could, in other words, serve the material and moral interests of both nations; what better tribute could be paid to the unique usefulness of the Utilitarian doctrine? Munro also held that the benefits of just laws and of moderate taxation were not enough unless an endeavour was made to raise the character of the natives. Elphinstone, like Munro, pleaded for a policy of gradualness in encroaching on the institutions of India. They were proposing a *via media* between Burkian conservatism and Benthamite radicalism, but they were closer in spirit to the former and in their programme to the latter. Elphinstone had great respect for Bentham but would not consider himself a Benthamite and wrote to Malcolm about how difficult it was to reconcile "Maratha Mamool with Jeremy Bentham". He also said of Babington, the President of the Regulation Committee, that "if he exceeds in any way, he does so in Benthamising".

There was a large, forward-looking conception of what they were trying to achieve among the utilitarians in India. Macaulay spoke with feeling about the pacific triumphs of reason over barbarism in the "imperishable empire of our arts and our morals, our literature and our laws". Western, especially English, education was the great panacea for the regeneration of India. Further, but for the abolition of Sati, Bentinck felt that he would be guilty of little less than "multiplied murder". Utilitarianism was not merely responsible for many reforms and material benefits by the middle of the 19th century; it introduced something more subtle and lasting. It spread a spirit of scepticism and curiosity, a willingness to judge every institution in terms of human reason and happiness, a spirit of innovation and social reform that required the initiative of the state for its fruition in a stagnant and decadent society, crippled by corrupt, pseudo-religious practices. It could even be argued that if the British ruling class needed the influence of Burke more than that of Bentham, the conquered Indian peoples needed the ideas of Bentham more than those of Burke, which were to some extent part of Indian tradition and thought. Unfortunately, the utilitarians were carried away by their conviction that they were replacing the iniquities of "Oriental despotism" in an inferior civilization by the benefits of benevolent despotism that came from a more enlightened nation. It was not so much a policy of continued interference that was adumbrated. It was an attitude of mind, a tone of voice that was so lacking in the sceptical spirit of utilitarianism except when directed at the beliefs and institutions of others. The culprit was chiefly James Mill and his weapon his highly overrated *History of British India*, but his complacency and insensitivity were common to the pundits if not the practitioners of utilitarianism. Mill singled out the Indians and the Chinese as particularly poor specimens of "uncultivated society", a far cry from the panegyrics they received in the 18th century from the thinkers of the Enlightenment. Hindu society, especially, was declared to be in such a hideous state that it was much inferior to Europe even in its darkest feudal age. And yet the utilitarians believed in the simple uniformity of human nature everywhere. This distorted and monotonously black picture of Oriental civilization that the utilitarians had became the basis of even more extreme claims by men like Balfour early in this century. Balfour declared that these great nations had got under the absolute government of the British "a far better government than in the whole history of the world they ever had before, and which not only is a benefit to them, but is undoubtedly a benefit to the whole of the civilized West". What was more, Balfour said in his Sidgwick Memorial Lecture[6] to Newnham that Oriental nations could never escape from their primeval despotism. "We may crystallize and re-crystallize a soluble salt as often as we please, the new crystals will always resemble the old ones." Even the "obscure disharmony between the Imperial system and the temperament of the West" was blamed on the East. The Imperial system "was perhaps too oriental for the occident, and it certainly became more oriental as time went on". Even Western decadence resultant upon Western imperialism could be blamed on Oriental despotism.

The utilitarians were preaching and practising in a climate of progress rather than of decadence; they had no serious qualms about being more authoritarian abroad than at home. They had not only taken social utility rather than tradition as the main criterion of social institutions and values. They also subscribed to a form of social determinism, to the results of forces that men are bound to accept one

[6] *Decadence*, 1908, pp. 35–41

day. Hence their political messianism, maintained by the convenient belief in an identity of interests between rulers and ruled. Determinism was combined with a form of historicism and messianism was enriched by an element of utopianism. It was the task of legislators to identify the interests of various groups, to reconcile them and thus reveal their inner identity. Good laws could make virtuous men. The rationalism that is implicit in utilitarianism was, of course, moderated by English empiricism and realism. The utilitarians made the exercise of absolute power subject to self-imposed rules, so that it ceased to be arbitrary and became dependable. A bridge was thus provided between the power-impulse of colonial administrators and Burke's exacting notion of moral responsibility. As Mill saw clearly, it was tempting to exercise vast power without commensurate responsibility in imperial territories; this was where utilitarianism came in handy. It was fortunate that the utilitarians in India did not sacrifice justice to utility or make utility so supreme that it displaced any independent notion of the good. If they did not generally bother about democracy or liberty, they were not alone in this respect. The doctrines of trusteeship and of utilitarianism had alike little use for representative institutions. Apart from this, the utilitarians were absurd rather than dangerous. Trustees could be solemn and utilitarians could be pompous. An extreme example was Macaulay, of whom Trevelyan wrote: "His topics, even in courtship, are steam navigation, the education of the natives, the equalization of the sugar duties, the substitution of the Roman for the Arabic alphabet in the oriental languages."

The utilitarians had their serious critics. Even the mid-century Radicals felt that the standard of utility was an intellectual concept too remote from the sentiment of the mass of people, whose relatives were toiling in oversea territories. At the same time utilitarians have been criticized for not going far enough, for not embarking on a more ambitious programme of social reform and of public works. Further, they have been attacked for their political materialism, for taking too narrow a view of happiness and being far more concerned with impersonal procedures and institutions than with the desires and dreams of men. Disraeli castigated what he called the "fallacy of supposing that theories produce circumstances" and of assuming that political institutions could be formed on abstract principles. The most reasoned criticism of utilitarian errors came from Maine on the basis of his sympathetic study of Indian society. He saw the injustice of

James Mill's treatment of Indian history and life and deprecated the tendencies towards imposed uniformity and centralization in a land of time-honoured usages and diverse local customs and declining village communities. The modern idea of legislation was alien to a society which denied law-making authority to its rulers, who were required to leave established social practices undisturbed. A blind adherence to abstract symmetry would only lead to practical confusion. Maine may have gone too far in his criticisms, but certain doubts and questions remain. Can an imperial authority exercised remotely through alien officials be properly aware of the wants, needs and the interests of the people? Can it ever take measures to promote the welfare of its distant subjects even at some sacrifice to domestic interests? How can imperial subjects be certain that references to the general interest of the Empire do not really mean only the interest of the ruling country? How to distinguish and decide between ephemeral interests and enduring sentiments or between current sentiments and long-term interests? These questions arise because an empire could never achieve in practice, perhaps not even in theory, the organic unity and the degree of social cohesion that might exist within a nation. These questions are easier asked than answered, but as to the continuing influence in India of the social reforms and the judicial and administrative and economic system that the utilitarians initiated there can be no doubt. The deeper consequence may well be their habit of endowing the rule of law with almost transcendental sanction, of securing for reason and utility the force of emotion and custom, of accepting rather than deploring the fact of political power and, above all, of showing that social change as well as stability is needed for happiness and social survival.

Whereas Burkean pragmatism was combined with a sure, firm sense of obligation, Benthamite utilitarianism, with its belief that political questions could only be treated by Baconian methods, was concerned with what was highly desirable rather than what was obligatory. Even in matters involving religious and moral principle, the utilitarians felt the need to consider consequences, balance probabilities, estimate forces and to choose the lesser evil. They were concerned in the sphere of politics with what was likely to do good or harm, not with what was definitely right or wrong, regardless of consequences. While the trustee took pride in his intentions and his sense of responsibility, the utilitarian relied on results and his sense of achievement. In Hindu terminology, the former stressed *Dharma* (duty), the latter emphasized *Artha* (interest). Both of these had been neglected in India owing to an obsession with *Moksha* (salvation), but the utilitarian doctrine was a greater blow to inertia than the doctrine of trusteeship was a shock to complacency. Indifference to the utilitarians was wholly impossible.

(vi)

It was Seeley who first saw most clearly that the British were not able to astonish the Hindu as easily as they thought. They simply must find an idea with the power to move men and to show that the British conquest was moral rather than material, representing the triumph of the modern over the medieval and the ancient world. Neither dutiful piety nor daring philanthropy could buttress the self-confidence of the rulers or bamboozle the ruled with their hoary culture as much as the heroic mission of spreading the light of the New Learning and the liberal gospel of progress. It was Jowett who showed how the Platonic doctrine of guardianship could be applied to India. In our own day Philip Woodruffe has elaborately used the Platonic model in his deeply felt, almost elegiac, apologia for the men who ruled India over the entire period of British domination. His book has been praised for not being like the "guilt-obsessed books" that distressed the reviewer in the *Sunday Times*.

In *The Republic* Socrates assures Thrasymachus that "there is no one in any rule who, in so far as he is a ruler, considers or enjoins what is for his own interest, but always what is for the interest for his subject or suitable to his art; to that he looks, and that alone he considers in everything he says and does". A careful selection must be made of those "who are the best guardians of their own conviction that what they think the interest of the state is to be the rule of their lives." It is necessary to safeguard against the watch-dogs turning upon the sheep and worrying them, behaving not like dogs but wolves; this was the task of the shepherds. They must receive such education as will have "the greatest tendency to civilize and humanize them in their relations to one another, and to those who are under their protection". They should not acquire so much property or wealth that they become housekeepers and husbandmen instead of guardians, enemies and tyrants instead of allies of the other citizens; "hating and being hated, plotting and being plotted against, they will pass their whole life in much greater terror of internal than of external enemies, and the hour of ruin, both to themselves and to the rest of the state, will be at hand". The guardians must be the smallest but the wisest of all classes in the state. The various classes should be kept from meddling with one another's occupations, as justice requires that no man is to have what is not his own. Injustice arises with the production of a state of things at variance with the natural order. Where there is no common but only private feeling a state is disorganized – when you have one half of the world triumphing and the other plunged in grief at the same events happening to the city or the citizens. In an ideal state the guardians are regarded as saviours and helpers by the people, while the rulers call the people their maintainers and foster-fathers. The entire state constitutes a single family. The ideal can never be perfectly realized, and at least there must be philosopher-kings who combine political greatness and wisdom, and who do not pander to popular whims. Governments vary as the dispositions of men vary, for states are made, not of oak and rock, but out of the human natures which are in them; the states are as the men are.

This, in essence, is the much-abused Platonic model which is attractive in terms of its own assumptions, and which Woodruffe regards as "an ideal model for the Indian system, not consciously adopted and exactly followed, for that is not the way English minds work". The English guardians were a small ruling class, an alien race, disinterested and aloof, "free from Platonic rigidity", with a real warmth for the Indian peasant, more concerned with peace and unity than with freedom, and by and large incorruptible. Their self-confidence was tempered by eccentricity, and such arrogance as they showed made them independent-minded. The despotic power they wielded was made bearable by the principle of delegation of authority coupled with full acceptance of personal responsibility. It was a despotism all the same, "as any system must be in which people are given what is good for them instead of what they want". These "amateur despots" were "expert in nothing or everything, answerable in practice mainly to themselves". The English guardians were confident that the Indian Brahmans of the 19th century were not at all like Plato's guardians and soon became convinced that they themselves were, for all their foibles such as pigsticking! Each generation was, according to Trevelyan, more simple, more hardy and more pious than the last. As they grew older, these guardians were not as uniform, sedate and forbidding as Plato's but were distinguished, according to Woodruffe, for "their diversity, their humanity, and their oddness". Thus the English guardians gave India a system that Englishmen would never have tolerated for themsleves.

Even if we accept Woodruffe's version of the Platonic model and his arguments to support the analogy, its implications for India must not be ignored. The advantages of the model were not only propagandist but also practical. It made a virtue out of the Prussian vice of self-glorification. It helped the ruling class and the ruling trace to believe in its mission and its destiny. It facilitated the education and the discipline of the civil service and rendered its members capable of cultivating their own gardens as well as those of others. It provided an impetus to public justice and to private integrity. It weakened potential opposition to the régime, at least partially and temporarily. Above all, it prevented open oppression and fostered minimum standards of fairness within the framework of a system that took despotic power and prestige for granted. It made it impossible for national pride to be subordinated to trading profits or for grand opportunities and exalted moral conceptions to be sacrificed to "the pure bread-and-butter doctrines of the political economists". Even the radicals like Bright were happier to be guardians than to be trustees or utilitarians.

Thanks to the guardians, Western education and culture were brought to india through a state directive rather than private initiative. If the guardians were aloof, so were their willing and unwilling wards alike; if they became an exclusive caste, they could claim to be following the example of the Hindus, including those who were eager for Western education. Apart from anything else, they did not mind – in fact almost took pride in – being disliked. The resentment of the Indians could, after all, be put down to a sense of inferiority and the antipathy of other nations could be attributed, as Professor Cramb[7] argued in 1900, to *phthonos*, Immortal Envy. The Platonic model was naturally sustained by the comforting belief that the British guardians were irreplaceable, as a class, by Indians. To put this on a permanent footing required the importation of a racial element into the Platonic model. Instinctive race prejudice had to be made doctrinal. Every native was regarded as incorrigibly corrupt or inherently inefficient or both. Lord Northbrook complained to Lord Dufferin that the Civil Service have strongly imagined that "no one but an Englishman can

[7] *The Origins and Destiny of Imperial Britain*

do anything". Sir John Strachey went so far as to claim hereditary virtues, mental powers and physical courage for the English, "those qualities necessary for the government of men, and which have given us an empire". The British guardians must always remain guardians because they alone possessed qualities that were proved by the fact that they were guardians, in the first place. These qualities unhappily did not render them safe from the absurdities of circular reasoning. J. A. Spender summed up fairly the attitude of the guardians. "The old-style Indian Civil Servant was an ideal guardian for an Indian Peter Pan. He brought with him the public school and Oxford and Cambridge tradition with all the excellent things that go with it – chivalry, courage, fair-play, self-confidence, the sense of responsibility, the habit of command and complete integrity. . . . Within the limits that he set to them his services were beyond praise, and India would be basely ungrateful if she forgot them. But he conceived himself as presiding over an eternal nursery which would never question his authority and always require the same services to be performed for it. He fought for this theory very gamely . . . But in the end he was his own undoing . . . the idea of governing a vast country of immense potential resources with a handful of public-school and university-trained men from another continent was bound to pass as soon as its people became conscious of their needs and had voices to express them". [8] When this happened, they complained that the policy of Indianization, like the grant of all political privileges, was looked upon by their rulers as a reward for good conduct rather than as a training in political character.

All these elements in the Platonic theory of guardianship as applied to India found expression, at least embryonically, in Jowett's letters. He wrote to Lansdowne in 1888 that "there is more opportunity of doing great and permanent good in India than in any department of administration in England, and the office having more power is also more free from the disagreeables of home politics". Old civil servants deplored to Jowett that crowds and congresses are so unmanageable. 'India for the Hindoo' was like 'Ireland for the Irish' and universal suffrage in England would not allow them to be coerced. Jowett felt that native character was "so different from the European that we hardly understand it". He regretted that "in India as in England we are apt to do things rather too late – so in Ireland". Jowett saw the difficulty of reconciling "the hopes of the natives and the suspicions of the

[8] *The Changing East*, 1926, pp. 154–5

English" but he felt that universal kindness and attention was the best basis of popularity. He did not believe that the congresses were really dangerous, as educated men who were not more than 1/10,000 were not really to be feared even if they secured English Liberal support and even if they were the most active and energetic of men. He suggested that a great deal could be done by securing the allegiance of the princes, by conferring benefits on the masses and admitting them to a "somewhat larger share of administration". But he warned that "whenever we admit them to Representation they will flood and drown us". He did not wish to deny that "the first duty of the English rulers of India is to maintain themselves", but couldn't the natives be conciliated without offending the civil service ? He felt that "the English and native tempers can never harmonize. The Englishman has no sympathy with other nations. He cannot govern without asserting his superiority. He has always a latent consciousness of the difference of colour." Was this a recognition that the theory of guardianship could not apply to the alien English in India? He had anyway a feeling that "a good-humoured ignoring" of the congresses was probably the right policy. "They should be treated with the greatest courtesy and even compliment, but of course, if they go beyond their tether, they have to be stopped." He was convinced that the precedents of the French Revolution or of the English Reform Bill were out of place in India, although to refuse any degree of representation was the height of inconsistency and also it was impossible to govern India without "a much larger infusion of the best natives".

The British, felt Jowett, should not be regarded as conquerors. They must create a common feeling between rulers and ruled for the good of India. There was a native wisdom beyond the traditions of the civil service and this must be tapped. When Jowett heard that there was trouble in India in 1891, he wrote that it was well not to lose time, for things move slowly. The phases of politics were, in his view, like the changes of weather and were always being forgotten. In 1892 he contended that the difficulty of India was social rather than political, as in England. As to the political question, he had asserted ten years earlier that it seemed to him that the Eastern must always be dependent on Western powers, "on England above all". Within a century, even Indian character might be visibly changed by education and mainly by material causes. There ought to be a good deal of Western supervision of Eastern officials, the one supplying honesty and justice, the other knowledge of the natives and aptitude for dealing with men. It was a pity that the best boys from the public schools were not being attracted in adequate numbers to the Indian Civil Service. On the whole, Jowett's political outlook is well brought out in a letter he wrote in 1892 on the condition of Russia which seemed to be very miserable. "Do you see any way of gradual improvement? Or are there impossibilities in the nature of things? To grant strict justice and toleration, not to Nihilists but to the Russian people in general, seems not an impossible thing even under a despotism. Cannot the Emperor be turned into what Plato calls a virtuous tyrant? . . . I believe that the Ambassador of a foreign nation may sometimes do for a people what they cannot do for themselves, because he sees the situation more clearly and he is trusted by the monarch when his own ministers are not – only as in so many other good things which have to be done he must not be found out doing them – or at any rate as in all difficult enterprises he must conciliate everybody and everything."

The real difficulty with the Platonic model was that it could be easily perverted by the Aristotelian notion that some men are born slaves and that the laws of freemen could never apply to them. The doctrine of guardianship had its charms for imperialists like Milner, who was much excited over the task of maintaining the *pax Britannica* among a fifth of the human race. It was not by what it took away but by what it gave that imperialism sought to win subject races to itself. Further, as Churchill said in 1926, "Once we lose confidence in our mission in the East . . . then our presence in those countries will be stripped of every moral sanction, and cannot long endure." But the fact remained that there could be no common will or purpose between an alien race and the ruled, and hence as Plato believed the state was bound to disintegrate. Guardianship was a grand ideal although unacceptable to a mature civilization, but no guardian could serve two masters or fulfil equally his two duties, to India and to England. Men like Gladstone were worried that England should take it on herself to act as the lawgiver, as foreigners were repelled by "too great a tendency to self-esteem – too little disposition to regard the feelings, the habits, and the ideas of others". The Platonic doctrine, however noble, could be corrupted by the Semitic notion of a chosen race as well as by a species of political Darwinism. Just as the revelations of Sinai and the promises of Jehovah did not concern the Gentile, the Gospel of 1688 could not be revealed except to Englishmen. The expansion of England

and the extent of the empire showed the survival of the fittest.

There were, of course, those who would not accept the doctrine of guardianship. When Frere became Member of the Viceroy's Council, he expressed his dislike of "a policy which puts all real power into the hands of European officials and European colonists and treats the natives as at best *in statu pupillari*, to be ruled, taught and perhaps petted, but to be excluded from all real power or influence . . . and to be governed . . . according to our latest English notion of what is best for them". Even Salisbury, when he was Secretary of State for India, in 1875 put his finger on the central weakness of the doctrine of guardianship. In a speech to the students at Cooper's Hill College, he said that "no system of government can be permanently safe where there is a feeling of inferiority or of mortification affecting the relations between the governing and the governed. There is nothing I would more earnestly wish to impress upon all who leave this country for the purpose of governing India than that, if they choose to be so, they are the only enemies England has to fear. They are the persons who can, if they will, deal a blow of the deadliest character at the future rule of England." [9] But, surely, was it not the height of unrealism to expect that this could be avoided when it was almost implicit in the theory and practice of guardianship and came to the fore when it was confronted with the bitter sense of alienation that wholly foreign rule produced? Salisbury himself gained a brief notoriety in 1888 by his slighting reference to Dadabhai Naoroji's election as M.P. for Finsbury – "I doubt if we have yet got to that point of view where a British constituency would elect a black man" – for which the Prime Minister was severely castigated by Morley and Gladstone and apparently admonished even by the Queen. It is indeed asking too much to expect missionaries of civilization and self-appointed guardians to mortify their feelings of national pride and racial prejudice or even to moderate their collective sense of superiority. Trustees may neglect their responsibility and utilitarians may abuse their power, but it is even easier for the guardians of the State to fail to be guardians of themselves, as Plato required them to be.

## (vii)

Burkean trusteeship, Platonic guardianship, even Benthamite utili-

[9] Sir Henry Cotton, *The New India*, 1904 edn., p. 42

tarianism could all become full-blooded theories that could justify and even sanctify British rule in India if a providential element could be imported into them. They could receive a supernatural sanction even if they were unable to secure popular acceptance or practical vindication or the gratitude of the natives. If the trustees could not be made accountable to a higher court of appeal on earth, they must at least be aware that they were answerable to God who had called them to their privileged position. The utilitarians, with all their wordly pretensions and their tendency to underrate human fallibility and sinfulness, could still be praised for their good works, which could be regarded as disguised acts of Christian charity. The utilitarian doctrine has even been described as a "side-wind from the main current of Christendom". The guardians could be more effective if they could feel that they were divinely appointed to perform the sacred mission of civilizing the lesser breeds without the law or holy writ. If only the Hindus and the rest could be regarded as superstitious and unregenerate, ignorant of the divine word and the divine will and therefore specially prone to sin and error, vice and corruption, it would be so much simpler to explain the extravagances of "Oriental stagnation", "Oriental despotism" and "Oriental backwardness".

It almost seems that if the evangelicalism of the Clapham sect, like the deity of Voltaire's universe, did not exist, it would have had to be invented. Fortunately, this was not necessary; evangelicalism flourished in its own right, even though it owed much of its impetus to the Indian connection. In fact, it existed before the other doctrines had been freely disseminated. Some have even assigned to Wilberforce rather than to Burke the credit for formulating the doctrine of trusteeship in regard to colonial possessions. This was convenient and generous in the past year, which was the bicentenary of his birth, and it could also be defended on the ground that by the abolition of slavery this great humanitarian rendered better services than Burke to the world as a whole. It is, in fact, indisputable that Burke formulated the doctrine of trusteeship more clearly and fully than anyone else, at any rate in England. But if Burke had greater influence on imperial administration, it was Wilberforce who really helped to create the British conscience in its attitude to colonialism. He once wished that the younger Pitt had resolved "to govern his country by *principle* rather than by influence". Wilberforce has been described as "that rare migrant into public life, the man of principle who achieves important practical results while always being labelled in his own day as an idealist rather than a politician". Although he invoked the wrath of Cobbett and the satire of Hazlitt, he could never be written off as a crank in the patrician society in which he had moved by right of talents. He made evangelicalism eminently, almost painfully, respectable in its time. His strength was rooted in a religious faith which came to him with revivalist suddenness and made him a zealot rather than a prig.

The Evangelical Movement was the result of the influence of Methodism on the Church of England. It became the Low Church of Anglican Methodism just as the Wesleyan sect was the High Church of Nonconformity. Hence the superior respectability of evangelicalism. It was pietist rather than rationalist, propagandist rather than conservative. It consisted of a Cambridge group under Isaac Milner and Charles Simeon and of the Clapham sect, which included the Thorntons, Zachary Macaulay, Lord Teignmouth, formerly Governor-General of India, James Stephen and John Venn. Their Calvinism was of a mild variety, and Wilberforce was very impressed with the unscriptural character of the Calvinistic system. The evangelicals were men of action and emotion who abstained from theological subtleties or speculations. Theirs was a sentimental and a practical Calvinism. They could work with Protestants of every domination, although they gradually persuaded themselves and others that they were the only true Christians. They could be petty as in their sneers at Coleridge. It is perhaps not surprising that they could not take to a thinker who asserted that he who set up Christianity over truth would end up by exalting his own sect above all others and by finally loving only himself. The evangelicals were, however, shallow and narrow rather than selfish and narcissistic. Evangelicalism, as Halevy pointed out, "constituted a link, effected a transition between Anglicanism and Dissent, between the governing classes and the general public, as represented by the great middle classes". It transmitted the gospel of duty and the panacea of education, while stressing the sovereignty of individual conscience and the possibility of sudden illumination resulting in total transformation.

The evangelicals were certain that British dominion in India was a divine dispensation, almost a miracle. Charles Grant's treatise of 1792 on the state of society and morals of Asiatic subjects and Wilberforce's own speeches showed that the evangelicals, unlike Burke, were only too ready to draw up an indictment against a whole people. Grant felt that the people of India were lamentably degenerate and base, yet obstinate in their disregard of what they knew to be right. He was shrewd in envisaging an Indian counterpart of the European Reformation, but he was small-minded in his contempt of everything in India, religions and laws, arts and crafts, manners and habits, morals and even misery. The evangelicals inevitably judged religious beliefs and development by worldly success and power. The elevation of Indian character could go hand in hand with the extension of British commerce, for was not this arrangement providentially provided? A community of interest between rulers and ruled could be established if India were anglicized. Wilberforce pleaded in Parliament that, owing to the "vast superiority even of European laws and institutions, and far more of British institutions, over those of Asia", the Indian community would only be too grateful to exchange "its dark and bloody superstitions for the genial influence of Christian light and truth" and to experience a substantial increase of civil order and security, of social pleasures and domestic comforts. The evangelicals had no doubts that they knew what was right and good for India as they knew what was right and good for England. They risked the imposition of English ideas on Indian soil because of their profound, almost touching faith that they were right. They took for granted that the heathen Hindoo in his darkness had to be enlightened by the English and meantime he had to be forced to abstain from what the light of gospel truth condemned.

The evangelicals, unlike some Englishmen of a later period, had no hesitations or reservations about the state of Western society or morality and really believed that they had nothing to learn from the East. They could not ever imagine a religious philosophy and mysticism that had nothing to do with the corrupt and repugnant social practices they saw or about which they heard gruesome stories. If they were sometimes prepared to consider a slower pace of reform and a less extreme form of interference, it was solely because they believed that undue haste would defeat its own ends and arouse the suspicions and animosity of the natives. There may have been differences of emphasis regarding tactics but there was not any doubt about the long-term strategy of the evangelical fanatics. They certainly could not countenance the early policy of non-intervention in religious matters of the East India Company.

Not only considerations of humanity or of moral obligation but the very progress of the Christian gospel and the success of the local missionaries required that Indian society should be rapidly renovated. There was a violent and desperate sense of urgency and little gentleness and humility among these zealots who wished to carry "the genial influence of Christian light and truth". Sir John Shore, or Lord Teignmouth, was prepared as Governor-General to connive at the activities of the first Baptist missionaries in Bengal in spite of their illegal entry into the country. This was not surprising in view of his solemn sense of professional obligation. "When I consider myself the Ruler of twenty-five millions of people, . . . I tremble at the greatness of the charge . . . I consider every native of India, whatever his situation may be, as having a claim upon me; and that I have not a right to dedicate an hour to amusement further than as it is conducive to health and so far to the despatch of business." He looked forward to the time "when I must render an account of my commissions as well as omissions", not to Parliament but to God. His successor, Wellesley, was less interested in evangelical work but was happy to tolerate missionary activities. Lord Minto had to implement a more cautious policy of religious non-intervention because of the Vellore mutiny but in time became increasingly liberal. His successors, Hastings and Amherst, felt they could not afford to risk disturbances, despite their personal regard for some missionaries. It was Bentinck's reforming policy that really fulfilled many of the intentions of the evangelicals.

Minto had complained against the "coarse and scurrilous invective against the most revered order of Hindu society", the threats of hell fire and damnation that had been bandied about in "the miserable stuff addressed to the Hindus" and confidently asserted that a just God will condemn no being without individual guilt. He was disturbed by missionary readiness to call out Atheism, Deism and persecution whenever a slip in their conduct had required to be rectified. Bentinck, on the other hand, was worried by Hindu rather than by missionary excesses. By abolishing an inhuman and impious rite such as sati, he felt that the Government would only be following, not preceding, the tide of public opinion. But he still remained aware of the dreadful consequences, in general, of a supposed violation of religious customs. At about the same time, Macaulay wrote to his father in 1836 that "if our plans are followed, there will not be a single idolater among the respectable classes of Bengal, thirty years hence". Yet a little over a decade earlier, Elphinstone had written, "To the mixture of religion

. . . with our plans . . . I most strongly object." But Macaulay's attitude of optimism was natural and consistent with the belief later on expressed by John Lawrence thus: "We are here by our moral superiority, by the force of circumstance, and by the will of Providence . . . in doing the best we can for the people we are bound by our conscience and not by theirs."

The real problem raised by the evangelical and messianic conception was not seen clearly until Lyall wrote in 1872 that the Government had not only to reconcile the interests and to recognize the peculiar institutions of several powerful native creeds radically distinct in structure and mutually hostile in temperament; it had also to submit its proceedings to tribunals of religious opinion in Europe as well as in Asia and "to take account of theological prejudices in two continents. So we are continually measured by inconsistent standards and weighed in discordant balances." A régime that prided itself on its individual and collective conscience and set before itself a lofty role of trusteeship had to contend with Hindu orthodoxy, Moslem iconoclasm, the refined Deism of the Brahmo Samaj, Nonconformist radicalism and the accusations of expediency and immorality levied by aggressive missionary societies.

Charles Kingsley defended the founders of the Brahmo Samaj against the criticism of more orthodox Churchmen. "I trust that no bigotry here will interfere with men who, if they are not at the point to which St Paul and St John attained, are trying honestly to reach that to which Abraham, David, and the Jewish prophets rose: a respectable height I should have thought." It was indeed fortunate that the British began to govern India at a time when religious excitement was at a low ebb at home, and were thus able to avoid the terrible extremes of fanaticism to which the Catholic nations of Europe had already gone. And yet British toleration could never mean a policy of perfect neutrality. If the Christian minority could not formally secure a sheltered position, if their opportunities for privileged access to the ears of the government could not be wholly relied upon, at least they could plead a policy of total disestablishment and dissociation from all religious institutions. But this only rendered the régime vulnerable to the Indian charge that it was wholly without any acceptable sanction, that it bore no relation whatever to the values held by the common people, that it was a satanic despotism despite its benevolent countenance, that it was an insupportable system of *Adharma*. The Mutiny of 1857 showed the

Government's dilemma; it was accused of treachery and deception and an attempt to entrap them into Christianity by those who rebelled; it was also regarded as divine chastisement for denying and degrading their own religion by missionaries and other fiercely puritanical laymen, many of whom had "a bias toward such combinations as the Bible and the sword". The British were even regarded as following in the Moghul tradition of pursuing and alternating between the incompatible policies of tolerance and conversion, vainly "reconciling the irreconcilable". Some evangelicals drew the conclusion that no Hindu or Moslem holidays should be observed, that all recognition to caste must be refused and that the Bible must be taught in all schools. Frere, on the other hand, felt no need for compromise as there was really no contradiction. "There can be no safe rule of guidance for a Christian Government different from that of a Christian individual – to do as we would be done by." And what Colonel Edwardes and others would wish to do "is just what we would ourselves resist to the death if attempted on us, – not by Hindoos or Moslems but by a Roman Catholic or Greek autocrat".

Later on in the Victorian period this note of religious impartiality was obscured and the evangelical element in British rule assumed a new and vulgar form. Kipling helped to secularize evangelism or at any rate to generalize it to cover almost everything. As Gustave Hervé[10] has well shown, patriotism becomes a full-fledged religion in its own right. The country becomes a kind of divinity whose name it is impious to pronounce irreverently. The priests of the new religion are the professional soldiers. With this goes a crude contempt for the patriotism as for the religions of other people; there is a fierce hatred of heretics and infidels. Patriotic songs replace hymns, text-books of history and civic education replace, or are combined with, the Bible and catechism, military costumes acquire the splendour of religious robes, religious "mummeries" are replaced by military exercises and parades, the flag is saluted with the same fervour shown to religious icons and sacraments. And yet the moral code of men like Kipling was essentially chaste as well as brutal, heroic as well as childlike. It was the religious coating that offended men like Joynson-Hicks who protested: "I know that it is said at missionary meetings that we have conquered India to raise the level of the Indians. That is cant. We conquered India by the sword, and by the sword we shall hold it. We hold it as the finest

[10] *My Country Right or Wrong*

outlet for British goods." But he exaggerated in his turn. The missionary spirit was "no mere sophism of unscrupulous imperialists" but a real emotion which would, of course, have horrified Warren Hastings.

The civilizing and christianizing role of the imperialists easily acquired the mystic character of a crusade – "save that, instead of the Cross, its banner is the pale pink tegument of the dominant race". Cromer thought that colour prejudice dated from the world-discoveries of the 15th century, one of the results of which was "to convince the white Christian that he might, not only with profit, but with strict propriety, enslave the black heathen". There were eminent divines who thought that the people of hot countries might be enslaved. Nicholas V issued papal bulls applauding the trade in negroes and hoped that it would end in their conversion. How did these notions enter into Protestant England of the late 19th century? They even led to acts that violated every religious canon, although ironically they were stimulated by an attitude of mind and a zeal that came originally from messianic, religious evangelism. Garratt courageously deplored "the long succession of murders and brutalities perpetrated by Englishmen upon Indians which either went unpunished or for which at the demand of the whole European community, only a small penalty was exacted". Sir Henry Cotton was also disturbed by the assaults of natives by Europeans that were of "frequent occurrence" and occasionally resulted in fatal consequences, while the trial of these cases "too often results in a failure of justice". These incidents were aberrations but they were based on commonly held maxims, that "the life of one European is worth those of many Indians", that "the only thing that an oriental understands is fear", and that England had been forced to lose many lives and spend many millions to hold India, for which she merited more substantial recompense than "the privilege of governing India in a spirit of wisdom and unselfishness". Many English youths looked with contempt on the creatures, "half-gorilla, half-negro", who appeared in Punch cartoons and regarded them as a "parcel of black heathen bodies and natives . . . worshipping sticks and stones, and swinging themselves upon bamboos like beasts". The noble humanitarianism of the early evangelicals thus tragically gave way to a vulgarized doctrine that caused much un-Christian brutality, no less evil than the un-Hindu cruelty of corrupt practices such as sati. Today we can see all this more clearly and impartially. It is significant that Lord Hemingford should pay a bicentenary tribute to Wilberforce in

Westminster Abbey by asserting; "We have no excuse for complacency: greed and injustice persist among all races; there are shadows and even stains on our record. But there are valid reasons for pride and thankfulness and many of them are directly or indirectly traceable to William Wilberforce, the great humanitarian, the father of the principle of trusteeship." [11]

Evangelicalism gave a sense of urgency, an intensity of zeal and a certain largeness of scope to British imperialism in India, lacking in the parish pump politics of little Englanders. It enabled imperialists to respond to the humanitarian impulse as well as to the missionary challenge, thus transmitting the humane spirit of the 18th century as well as the dour Puritanism and harsh Calvinism of earlier periods to England and its empire in the 19th century. It meant that a definite moral imperative and an ethical idea of imperial service were laid upon what otherwise might have been merely a mixture of commercialism and exploitation. Evangelicalism was elastic enough, for all its grim rigidity, to provide the basis for a campaign for the physical emancipation of slaves as well as for a crusade to justify the political enslavement of freemen. Its real weakness was that it assumed that "all the giving and serving, all the responsibility and all the sacrifice are on one side, and all the need, all the receiving, all the gratitude (if any) are on the other". Further, the evangelical imperialists took risks that they had perhaps no right to take, they did not see that "the axioms of Clapham were paradoxes in Calcutta", and they could not imagine that "a time comes when the divine mandate is exhausted, and then a change must be made, for the virtue has gone out of the work and both parties will suffer".[12] They were more successful in anglicizing than in christianizing India. Even the extent of effective anglicization has been doubted. Sir Henry Lawrence wrote in 1932: "I used to hear of India being 'Anglicized'; but in my experience it was rather the other way. It was we who were being Indianized. I never met an Anglicized Indian. I saw and knew many who spoke and dressed like Englishmen; but they will never be English. They have too much to lose and to leave, and the ancestral mortmain grips them. It would be far easier for the detached Englishman to become Indian. For we went to India at a most plastic and impressionable age . . ." [13]

[11] *The Times*, August 25, 1959

[12] William Paton, *The White Man's Burden*, 1939, p. 55

[13] *Fifty Years*, 1882–1932, a symposium, p. 164

The reasons for the failure of christianization were seen by some administrators as well as missionaries. Cotton came to the view that as the Hindu mind naturally runs in a religious groove, its instinct is to recoil from any bold solution of its present moral difficulties which does not arise from the past religious history of the nation. At best, their attitude was but a compromise between Rationalism and Hinduism. Dr Congreve tried to show why Christianity could not make any deep impression on the two powerful systems of Brahminism and Mahometanism. "If in his contact with Brahminism the missionary puts forward the philosophical side of Christianity, the subtle mind of the Brahmin delights in the combat, and meets him with a counter-philosophy. There is matter for endless dispute, but there is no result. If more wisely advised, the missionary rests on the simple statements of Christianity, on the facts of its history and its appeal to the conscience of men, he spares himself personally the annoyance of defeat in argument, or the pain of seeing his arguments make no impression, but for his cause the effect is the same. For the religious system of India leaves its worshippers no sense of want . . . The contest is not such as it was with the polytheistic systems of Greece and Rome. . . . On Mahometanism Christianity has made no impression, has tacitly renounced the attempt to make any. The rival Monotheisms met in the middle ages . . . Greek Christianity succumbed. Latin Christianity waged successfully a defensive war . . . Each of the rivals claims for itself an exclusive possession of the religious belief of mankind. Both alike are rejected by the other. They rest side by side, convincing monuments of the exaggeration of their respective claims." [14]

Although evangelicalism failed to achieve its ends, it left its wider influence behind. Even if Christianity did not make many converts, its secularized expressions as well as the challenge of conversion itself stimulated and affected Indian thought and life. But the chief impact of evangelicalism was on the doctrines of Burkean trusteeship, Benthamite utilitarianism and Platonic guardianship. There were also other Christian elements besides evangelicalism, especially the notion of "penitence for the sins of our forefathers, with an anxious desire to expiate, if possible, their fault", but essentially a silent sense of duty and a profound conception of personal responsibility. But these other elements, however important, did not constitute a doctrine; they existed in spite of all the theories and reflected the influence of religion

[14] Quoted by Sir Henry Cotton, *The New India*, p. 228

and morality on Victorian lives. The evangelicals were able to modify as well as to affect the other doctrines. Their belief that legislation was powerless to change human character was an antidote against utilitarian legalism; their faith in anglicization undermined the Burkean veneration for tradition and custom in India; their view of education as a universal panacea was opposed to the hierarchical notion of a Platonic *élite*. On the other hand, the evangelical zeal for reform, consciousness of destiny and sense of mission provided stimulation to the utilitarians, the trustees and the guardians, although at different times the evangelicals came closest to each of the others.

(viii)

The interaction between the four doctrines was too subtle and complex to be reduced to any simple scheme or stable relationship. There were affinities as well as contradictions between all of them, but collectively they had continuing force and even a strange unity that could not have come to the political theory of imperialism merely through any two, or even three of them. Although at different times different doctrines predominated even to the apparent exclusion of what were once rival theories, all the four elements were there in some form or the other, from the beginning to the end. It was natural that trusteeship should appeal especially to the British Parliament, utilitarianism to the imperial government in India, guardianship to the civil service and evangelicalism to non-official bodies and societies. More generally, Burke provided a moral code, Bentham a programme, Plato an attitude of mind, and Wilberforce a transcendental sanction and a belief in oneself. All these were somehow needed in the solemn business of ruling over a long period in a distant country and among a vast and alien people, thus combining philanthropy and profit, conscience and convenience, expediency and dogma, prejudice and pride. The feeling for principle had somehow to come to terms with the facts of power, while reason had to serve as well as to restrain emotion. It was not always easy, even in practice let alone in theory, to unite the four doctrines.

Benthamite utilitarianism stresses the idea of happiness as against the idea of duty, results rather than intentions, "moral legislation" rather than "moral pathology". The word *utile*, the useful, has carried with it a double antithesis and been contrasted with the *honestum*, the worthy or honourable, and the *dulce*, the agreeable or the attractive. Bentham himself felt that "utility", which he borrowed from Hume, was an unfortunately chosen word as the idea it gives was "a vague one". The British imperialist could never consciously prefer the *utile* to the *honestum* even though he could often choose it against the *dulce*. The other three doctrines saw to this. Bentham himself recognized the "constant responsibility" of trustees as well as "the strictest and most absolute dependence" on their creators. He also appreciated the role of the guardians in relation to "the untaught and unlettered multitude", though he went too far for the imperialists in wanting the multitude "to occupy themselves without ceasing upon all questions of government (legislation and administration included) without exception . . ." Of course, the Benthamite contempt for custom could never be reconciled with Burke's veneration, although Bentham could concede the occasional usefulness of custom.

Burke had reacted against the rationalism of the *philosophes* and the nascent utilitarianism of Bentham. It is no less difficult to reconcile Burke with the conservative utilitarianism of Paley than with the radical utilitarianism of Bentham or what has been miscalled the revolutionary utilitarianism of Godwin. The moral state of mankind filled Burke with dismay and horrors. "The abyss of Hell itself seems to yawn before me." He felt that "nothing can be conceived more hard than the heart of a thorough-bred metaphysician. It comes nearer to the cold malignity of a wicked spirit than to the frailty and passion of a man. It is like that of the principle of evil himself, incorporeal, pure, unmixed, dephlegmated, defecated evil." This was, of course, directed against the abstractions and metaphysical presuppositions that he did not share or accept implicitly. But in this respect Burke was more typically British than Bentham and, therefore, more influential. The British are nothing if not empirical as they take their own metaphysics of common sense for granted, but the British imperialist administration could not dispense with the need which the Prusso-German bureaucracy heartily welcomed, the need for "a metaphysical smoke screen". Benthamite utilitarianism was far more than this and entered into practical programmes even while the Burkean spirit was never lost. This was because the Burkean doctrine could appear too static a concept of empire, a majestic posture of masterly inactivity, and at different times the need was felt for a dynamic force, a new vitality in imperial rule. But the supreme merit and use of the Burkean doctrine, against all considerations of reason and utility, was that it provided the decisive argument in favour of the given system, as against all imaginable conceptions of a future which is no more than possible – that is *exists* and that it is the necessary consequence of the past. Further, Burke was famous while Bentham was still obscure; the prophet got in before the pamphleteer. The Burkean doctrine went so deep that it later on modified the Platonic one. The guardians were required to wield their power by delegating it while at the same time assuming full responsibility for everything because of their private conviction that each had made a pact with his country and with God.

Burke and Plato combined to set before the administration extremely high standards by which it was inevitably found to be wanting by Englishmen as well as by Indians. This is not so much a pointer to dishonesty and deceit as a proof of pride and high idealism, of spiritual ambition as well as an exalted ethic. The Burkean doctrine was easier to invoke than the Platonic was to justify the withholding of representative institutions which could train the wards and treat them as pupils in representative government. On the other hand, the Platonic doctrine was more easily perverted by the poison of race prejudice than the Burkean doctrine. The Platonic doctrine could be used to combat every notion of equality. The Burkean doctrine could show the awful conflict between the "pseudo-liberalism" of granting representative government and the staid conservatism of permanently retaining trusteeship. Race prejudice came later than the opposition to representative institutions and reinforced it. Men like Mayo and Lawrence, Canning and Dalhousie, were against any distinction of class or race. Lawrence even appreciated the role of trustees in regard to self-governing institutions. In 1864 he said: "The people of India are quite capable of administering their own affairs; the municipal feeling is deeply rooted in them. The village communities, each of which is a little republic, are the most abiding of Indian institutions. Holding the position we do in India, every view of duty and policy should induce us to leave as much as possible of the business of the country to be done by the people." This view was naturally rare.

The four doctrines had been united by the view, chiefly spread by the evangelicals, that India was no good for anything, and seemed to enjoy tyranny. Even Macaulay had said that it would be as absurd to establish popular governments in certain countries as "to abolish all the restraints in a school or to unite all the strait-waistcoats in a madhouse". And yet later on the Burkean and Platonic doctrines could combine to enable imperialism to take credit even for the nationalism that it unwittingly created. In the 20th century, the "theory of decolonization" originally put forward by socialist imperialists like Ramsay MacDonald could be assimilated into the political theory of British imperialism in Asia. The four doctrines could be made to serve different purposes at different times. In the latter part of the 19th century they could be given a Hobbesian coating. Stephen had said that "earth resembles heaven in one respect at least. Its kingdom suffereth violence, and the violent take it by force." Austin was always worried that political or civil liberty had been erected into an idol by "doting and fanatical worshippers". Stephen and Austin were thinking of England and not only the empire.

In 1886 Lord Dufferin, a year after the birth of the Indian National Congress with his consent, had reiterated the role of the government as "an isolated rock in the middle of a tempestuous sea, around whose base the breakers dash themselves simultaneously from all the four quarters of the heavens". This view was a constant theme throughout the duration of the British Empire in India. There was the idea that Indians respected power, that they could easily be intimidated by force. There was also the British pride in being disliked, a sense of achievement in indifference to popular demands. The four doctrines resulted in the supreme paradox that the imperial rulers, who could not put their trust in princes or in politicians, in the old feudal or the new professional classes, unintentionally helped to democratize India, while adhering to their own polite form of autocratic government. Only the aliens could give good government to a disunited country and only they could be compelled to grant self-government to a united nation. All four doctrines were held with utmost sincerity, which the cynics who claim superior honesty, can deny only at the expense of truth. All four doctrines were abused as well as misinterpreted, which the apologists who claim superior knowledge, can deny only at the expense of justice.

(ix)

It is important that we should not ignore that other elements existed besides these four doctrines or that British rule in India went through a baffling variety of phases. The four doctrines do not go to make up a symphony; there were too many discordant notes, too many jerks and surprises, too many disagreeable noises. If there was a symphony, it sounded at times as if it could have been by Beethoven and at other times as if it was by Bartok. In any case, it was a form of music to which few Indians could respond. Warren Hastings had enunciated the need to combine power with responsibility, the need for strong as well as good government, the need to rule according to Indian customs, the need to protect the customary rights of the ryots, the need for centralized and direct control over all British dominions in India. He had urged in 1772 the necessity of experiment. "We must adopt a plan upon conjecture, try, execute, add, and deduct from it, till it is brought into a perfect shape." The next year he criticized not his predecessors but rather "the want of a principle of government adequate to its substance, and a coercive power to enforce it". In 1804 Wellesley felt that "the position in which we are now placed is suited to the character of the British nation, to the principles of our laws, to the spirit of our constitution, and to the liberal and comprehensive policy, which becomes the dignity of a great and powerful empire".

In the intervening period between Hastings and Wellesley there had been the attempt of Cornwallis to impose his Whig conception of English landed society and to create an Indian aristocracy. Teignmouth had come to the view that "if we should confer happiness upon them, it will be in spite of themselves". With his evangelical sympathies, he naturally felt: "Every hour I stay in this country, my situation becomes more irksome . . . The knowledge, such as it is, which I have acquired of the people, their customs and manners, does not make me like them the better." Minto who followed Wellesley reaffirmed the declared principle to protect the followers of each religious system in "the undisturbed enjoyment of their respective opinions and usages; neither to interfere with them ourselves, nor to suffer them to be molested by others". It was important to establish a system of administration best calculated to promote the confidence and conciliate the feelings of the natives, not less by a respect for their own institutions, than by the endeavour gradually to engraft upon them such improvements as might communicate to every class of people, under the safeguard of equal laws, "that sense of protection and assurance of justice, which is the efficient spring of all public prosperity and happiness".

With Bentinck there came a determination to found "British Greatness upon Indian Happiness", to inaugurate the age of reform and to curb "barbarous excesses" by legislation as well as by education. Munro went further and hoped that "we shall in time so far improve the character of our Indian subjects as to enable them to govern and protect themselves". Elphinstone, on the other hand, was concerned that "we have dried up the fountains of native talent, and that from the nature of our conquest not only all encouragement to the advancement of knowledge is withdrawn, but even the actual learning of the nation is likely to be lost, and the productions of former genius to be forgotten". When we come to Dalhousie, "a Scotsman bred on the Shorter Catechism", we meet with the postulate that it was not only the right but the duty of the paramount power to lose no legal opportunity of suppressing dependent states and substituting its own direct rule, of suppressing native usages and practices where they seemed to be barbarous and establishing the entire apparatus of Western civilization.

The tragedy of the Mutiny came as a shock to the complacency of the rulers, and it was followed by the Queen's proclamation eschewing racial discrimination and religious intolerance and affirming the obligation to maintain "the ancient rights, usages and customs of India". In the sixties Lord Lawrence felt that "great public benefit is to be expected from the firm establishment of a system of municipal administration in India". Earlier, Frere had hoped that there would be a large and an increasing school of officials "who hold with Hastings and Cornwallis, Wellesley, Malcolm and Montstuart Elphinstone rather than with Lord Dalhousie and Mr Thomason and the later school of levelling, resumption and annexation". In fact, British rule during the remaining period was more ambivalent than ever, with sharp contrasts between Lytton and Ripon, Dufferin and Curzon, Reading and Irwin. In England itself, there was the fierce antagonism between Gladstone and Disraeli. Gladstone talked of the imperial mission to shed the light of liberty on other lands, while Disraeli asserted plainly that self-governing colonies were a contradiction in terms and that the empire was a proud and permanent possession that lent a living prestige to the British heritage. Others argued that Britain, as the country which understood liberty best, had a unique right to rule over other peoples and races. Cromer declared that it would probably never be possible to make a Western silk-purse out of an Eastern sow's ear. Lyall could even plead that "Indian spirituality is against the ideas and institutions of self-government".

With Curzon came the plea that official and non-official Englishmen should stand together and not reproduce ever again the mutual animosity that came to a head with the Ilbert Bill under Ripon's viceroyalty. Addressing the mine-owners at Burrakur, he declared: "My work lies in administration, yours in exploitation." Mill's warnings that the English in India must be either administrators or exploiters were forgotten or spurned. After Curzon the spirit of liberalism asserted itself again, but Morley could write to Minto, "Not one whit more than you do I think it tenable or possible or even conceivable to adapt English political institutions to the nations who inhabit India". This "hierophant of liberalism" suspected that what the political classes in India "really want a million times beyond political reforms is access to the higher administrative posts of all sorts". The demand for freedom was despised as a cloak for crude ambition. In 1910 Ramsay Macdonald asserted that "efficiency is not better than self-government". In 1920 he declared that "unless the British political genius is to change fundamentally for the worse, the British conquest is to issue in liberty and self-government". This had already been argued by the Round Table Group of Lionel Curtis, and Chelmsford came under this influence. He and Montagu felt that the desire for self-determination was the inevitable result of education in the history and thought of Europe.

Later on, the Report on Indian Constitutional Reform combined a theory of political liberalism with a doctrine of active state intervention. It declared that "English theories as to the appropriate limits of state activity are inapplicable in India and that if the resources of the country had to be developed the Government must take action". The wheel had come full circle. The triumphant utilitarianism of the exponents of a theory of enlightened despotism in the early decades of the 19th century now returned under the guise of a new conception of state socialism. This was used, together with the exigencies of war, the Burkean conception of trusteeship adapted to the interests of minorities, as well as the inability of the Platonic guardians to grow up and face the facts of life around them, to delay the consummation that had been envisaged by Munro, Elphinstone and even by Macaulay. In the end it had to come. The evangelicalism of the past had gone and the doctrines of Burkean trusteeship, Benthamite utilitarianism and Platonic guardianship had lost their ancient flavour and authentic fervour. Anachronistic survivals like Lieut.-Colonel Wyllie[15] of the Indian Army and the India Defence League ranted in vain against

[15] *India at the Parting of the Ways – Monarchy, Diarchy, or Anarchy?* 1934

"the dreamers, dogmatists and defeatists" among their own compatriots. The willingness of the English spirit prevailed over the weakness of its imperial flesh.

The diversities among the men who ruled India and the contradictions between the various doctrines that they invoked must not make us forget the nature of the system that was set up and eventually had to be abandoned. It was a centralized, enlightened despotism that was transformed in time into an elaborate, autocratic bureaucracy. The despotism was softened by a spirit of tolerance, the bureaucracy was tamed by a tradition of equity. The Government of India was described by Lytton as a "government by despatch-box tempered by an occasional loss of keys". Like every despotism, it was based on the principle that everything had to be done for the people as they could do nothing themselves. There was sometimes, as under Curzon's rule, a tension between personal autocracy and the collective bureaucracy.

As the system lacked any principle of justification that derived from the beliefs and values of the people over whom it ruled, it was often induced to support its policies by the simple plea of *raison d'état*. Apart from power-oriented notions of authority, the utility of non-material incentives to the men who administered the system was fully recognized and largely met; they had to, and were helped to, believe in themselves. Utilitarianism was implicit in the system and compensated for the highly inadequate degree of communication between the ruling *élite* and the various social classes in the country. The system required a class of interpreters, a class of persons "Indian in blood and colour but English in tastes, in opinions, morals and intellect", but these interpreters became either ineffective or inconvenient as a class. They either lost touch with their own people or were not content to go on being disloyal to them. The system created economic as well as social and cultural problems that it could not solve. Agrarian and industrial revolutions were begun but could not work themselves out fully or fruitfully under the conditions of imperial rule. There were inevitable contradictions inherent in the system. There could not be any harmony of political aims or cultural ends between the rulers and the ruled. The centralized system had to be maintained by a policy of 'divide and rule' even if some thought it to be the only way of ensuring fairness to all social and religious groups. It could not carry out its duties both to the British nation and to the Indian people with equal ease. It was naturally prone to inertia, to follow the maxim of Mendoza, the first

Viceroy of new Spain: "Do little and do that slowly."[16] Hence Jowett's complaint that it had become an English habit to do the right thing in the wrong way, to do too little and to do it too late. Every centralized bureaucracy is, in a sense, a failure, but especially so if it is administered by an alien people. Often, the wrong thing was done in the right way rather than the other way about because what the system lacked by its very nature was partly supplied by the moral code and personal qualities of the men who ran the system.

## (x)

It is easy to see why Indian nationalists concentrated their attack on the system rather than on the men who administered it, especially after Gandhi came along to show that this was required by Indian religious ethics and tradition. Before him it was common to attack the men for their inability to carry out their own high standards, to take their political beliefs on their face value. But at different times the four main doctrines of British imperialism were challenged by Indian nationalists, quite apart from their attack on the system. In the early decades of the 19th century, Metcalfe had written, "All India is at all times looking out for our downfall". Bentham at the same time referred to Ram Mohan Roy as his "intensely admired and dearly beloved collaborator in the service of mankind".

Roy was very impressed by Bentham's notion of the duty of resisting the Government in case the benefit to be secured by this is greater than the evil of revolution. He said, "If mankind are brought into existence, and by nature formed to enjoy the comforts of society and the pleasure of an improved mind, they may be justified in opposing any system, religious, domestic or political, which is inimical to the happiness of society or calculated to debase the human intellect." He also believed that enemies to liberty and friends of despotism have never been and never will be ultimately successful. Democracy and imperialism were incompatible, but it was better to rely on the enlightened public opinion of England than to be governed by a bureaucratic legislature. Ranade, on the other hand, who was born almost a decade after Roy's death, combined a Burkean view of the State with a Benthamite theory of social reform, and also had his own belief in India as a chosen race and challenged the British claim to be a superior

[16] R. Syme, *Colonial Elites*, 1958, p. 60

caste of eternal guardians. The State in its collective capacity "represents the power, the wisdom, the mercy and charity of its best citizens". He preached a philosophy of moderation and liberalism, stressing the need for justice between man and man, giving to the rulers the loyalty that is due to the law they are bound to administer but securing at the same time to the ruled the equality which is their right under the law. He was prepared to accept foreign interference in social matters on utilitarian grounds that were different from those that had been used by the Benthamites like Bentinck. Ranade shrewdly argued that the foreign rulers have no interest to move of their own accord. "If they consulted their selfish interests only, they would rather let us remain as we are, disorganized and demoralized, stunted and deformed, with the curse of folly and wickedness paralyzing all the healthy activities and vital energies of our social body. The initiation is to be our own, and based chiefly upon the example of our venerated past, and dictated by the sense of the most representative and enlightened men in the community." He pleaded that the foreigners were merely giving the responsible sense of progressive Indian thinkers the force and sanction of law in matters such as sati and infanticide and the recognition of the validity of widow marriages.

Benthamite utilitarians were unwittingly serving the cause of Hindu tradition and the stability of Hindu society, which Burke respected, by their reforms. They helped to bring about a Hindu renaissance and a Hindu reformation rather than a total revolt against religious tradition, let alone a massive conversion to Christianity. As Ranade said, "the change is sought not as an innovation, but as a return and restoration to the days of our past history. Those who advocate it justify it on the authority of texts revered, and admitted to be binding to this day. The intermediate corruption and degradation was not of the nation's seeking. It was forced upon it by the predominance of barbarous influences, and by the intolerance of ruthless conquerors." If men like Balfour could later on argue that Western decadence was caused by oriental despotism and imperialist ideas imported from the East, Ranade was convinced that Indian decadence, which no one could doubt, was caused by Moghul despotism and British imperialism. He, too, like the evangelicals in England, had his own notions of divine dispensation and Hindu pride. "It was not for nothing that God has showered His choicest blessings on this ancient land of Aryavarta. We can see His hand in history. Above all other countries we inherit a civilization and a religious and social polity which have been allowed to work their own free development on the big theatre of Time."

The liberal, utilitarian and Burkean elements in Ranade's thought were directly transmitted to Gokhale in Poona, while the exclusive and providential element was independently pushed to violently messianic extremes in Calcutta by men like Vivekananda and Aurobindo. Ranade's direct answer to Benthamite utilitarianism took the form of a special theory of Indian economics which was combined with a theory of imperialist exploitation – the "Drain Theory" – of Dadabhai Naoroji, put forward long before Ranade wrote, in 1870.

All this represent a marked change since the thirties in Bengal, when Western doctrines were uncritically accepted and could not, therefore, be turned against British imperialism, despite the splendid example set by Roy, whom Ranade regarded as one of India's greatest men. Roy was a universalist in religious but not in secular matters and could not accept the Benthamite notion that there were universal principles that could be applied to legal codes everywhere. Of course, he cherished the Indo-British connection as a decisive step towards universal brotherhood. The young Bengali intellectuals of the thirties, however, were not only good loyalists but also blind imitators. "In matters of politics, they are all radicals and are followers of Benthamite principles", commented *The Englishman* in 1836. A critic of secular education like Tarachand got Benthamism upside down and pleaded for moral education "which recognizes, above all, the grand deontological maxim of Bentham, that a man's duty to do, cannot but be also his interest". The period between Roy in Bengal and Ranade in Bombay, between the thirties and the nineties, saw many drastic changes of thought that were achieved through a confusing variety of phases. In 1858 Harishchandra Mukherjee, in an article in *The Hindu Patriot*, asserted that the time had nearly come when all Indian questions must be solved by Indians. The emergence of the educated middle class as a new force had upset the old equilibrium of the constitution between the Civil Service, the supreme court and the *zamindars*, the three estates of the Indian realm. Soon the influence of Montesquieu and Bentham gave way to that of Buckle and Mill. In 1873 Asutosh Mukherjee stoutly defended Mill against the attack of Fitzjames Stephen, and also criticized Austin's theory of sovereignty. "How long and how often is obedience to be rendered in order that it may be habitual?" he asked. Jogendranath Vidyabhushan, on the other hand, quoted Charvaka to prove the fraudulent character of the ancient Brahmins. He believed that the Positivism of Comte was the coming religion of the world.

In 1883 Saurindramohan Tagore wrote a book, *Hindu Loyalty*, quoting ancient Indian texts in support of loyalty to Queen Victoria. Nabagopal Mitra agreed with Mill that despotism was more suited to India at the time than representative government, but felt a monarchy was a lesser evil than an oligarchy of foreigners. Sisirkumar Ghosh, however, felt that India had become fit for a democracy and had passed the tribal and then the centralizing or despotic phase that every nation must pass through. Imperialism, he felt, was harmful not only to the conquered but also to the conqueror. It was really Bankimchandra who effectively tried to reinterpret Indian political ideas in the light of Western thought and to convert the political theory of British imperialism into the political theory of Indian nationalism. He found traces of Benthamite utilitarianism in the Indian epics and in the *Bhagavad-Gita*, but he felt that it only accounted for a part of Dharma. He was also influenced by Mill's individualism and Comte's *Religion of Humanity*. He became directly concerned with the two essential elements in nationalism, the method of identification of the individual interest with the welfare of a particular community, and the method of differentiation of the interest of the particular community from other communities. Neither of these elements had been present in India, with its extreme individualism combined with an exacting universalism. He felt that the only way to achieve results was to exalt patriotism to the dignity of a religion by relating it to the love of humanity. His entire doctrine of nationalism was taken over by Bepin Chandra Pal and Aurobindo Ghosh, whose messianic fervour was more directly fed by the message of Vivekananda, who passionately pleaded that India, with its unique mission and destiny, must once more conquer the world through its religious philosophy and its spirituality. "There is no other alternative, we must do it or die."

The methods of Indian nationalists, in their challenge to the theory of British imperialism, were of marked variety. There was the appeal to British qualities of fair-play and justice, a method used by the early "moderates" as well as by Naoroji, co-founder of the Congress, who ended up as an "extremist". There was the challenge to the imperialist doctrines on the basis of other elements in Western political thought, the invoking of Paine against Burke and natural rights against the duties of trustees, of Mill against Bentham and representative democracy against utilitarian despotism, of Mazzini against Plato and national destiny against imperial guardianship, equality under natural law against the special claims of the evangelicals. There was the attack on the system on theoretical as well as practical grounds and on some of the men who represented its inherent vulnerability. Finally, there was the Gandhian challenge to British behaviour, theory and the system in terms of Indian ethical standards, political and religious conceptions, and national aspirations. Burke had written that "a kind of Providence has placed in our breasts a hatred of the unjust and cruel in order that we may preserve ourselves from cruelty and injustice". Naoroji echoed this sentiment when he said in 1869 that the Englishman is incapable of despotism. "He might, and often did, carry things with a high hand, but the instinct and love of liberty, the constitutionalism which is born with and ingrained in him, made him at the time of trial recoil from being stigmatized a despot." Indians should have a parliament in India as their goal, but meantime the educated had to play the role of Platonic guardians and educate the people to prepare them for representative institutions. In 1882 Naoroji was deeply rooted in his "Drain Theory" but wrote to Hyndman about his hope of results if the English labouring classes could be moved, and about the need for "educating England in the great Indian question". He was despondent because "the Liberals seem to be eating their own words. The feeling of despair comes over me sometimes, but perseverance is absolutely necessary. For efforts in a right cause the result sometimes comes when least expected." If the present material and moral destruction of India continued, however, a great convulsion must inevitably arise, unless an English statesman arose to do "what the world should expect from English conscience, and from England's mission to humanity".

Naoroji soon became pained by the contradiction between English constitutionalism at home and liberalism in Europe, on the one hand, and her "despoiling despotism in India under a pseudo-constitutionalism", on the other. The English were descending to "the lower level of Asiatic despotism", a concept that Naoroji borrowed from English writers. In 1897 Naoroji, a deeply disillusioned man, roundly declared that "the unrighteous and un-British system of government" was responsible for "an unceasing and ever-increasing bleeding" of India and was "maintained by a political hypocrisy and continuous subterfuges, unworthy of the British honour and name, and entirely in opposition to the wishes of the British people". Disaster to the empire would be the inevitable result. This was a recurring theme in Congress Presidential Addresses.

At this time many Indian nationalists were convinced that the era of mendicancy, of petitions and moral appeals, was finally to be ended. Just as imperialists believed that the Oriental only respects power, so many nationalists now declared that the Occidental and particularly the hypocritical and moralizing British could only understand the language of force and the concreteness of organized violence. This meant the force of words as well as of arms. There was no more question of claiming freedom. "Swaraj is our birthright," declared Tilak. Paine's powerful attack on Burke was widely read and deeply absorbed. Man had no property in man, the authority of the dead could not be invoked against the rights and the freedom of the living. No nation had a divine right to rule over another. A revolt was proper against "the despotism of principles" rather than of men. The imperialists venerated power and not principles. There was no "monopoly-government of wisdom" of wise men of Gotham, of Platonic guardians. The masses could not be looked upon as a herd of beings that must be governed by fraud, effigy, and show. The principle of trusteeship was false because it presumed to renounce the rights of all posterity in the name of fictitious obligations to dubious ancestors.

In 1930 the Congress adopted a resolution in favour of Purna Swaraj, or complete independence, which spoke the language of Paine with the detachment and calm dignity of Gandhi. Gandhi inherited the tradition of Gokhale, whom he regarded as his guru, as well as that of Tilak. At a time when the "extremists" were inclined to use the arguments of Paine in conjunction with the wholly different principle that the end justifies the means, that flavoured of the notorious English pamphlet of 1657 by Colonel Sexby (*Killing No Murder*), Gokhale, the greatest of the "moderates", spoke with the political outlook of Burke and the moral fervour of Bright. He appreciated the temporary role of Platonic guardians but firmly rejected the principle of State landlordism. He appealed to the trustees to do their duty under a sense of self-restraint as they did not yet have to contend with the power of the electors as in England. In 1902 he pleaded the need for a Government, national in spirit though foreign in personnel. He contrasted the narrower imperialism based upon race superiority with "that nobler Imperialism which would enable all who are included in the Empire to share equally in its blessing and honours". But

Gokhale, like Naoroji had done earlier, stiffened in his attitude during the viceroyalty of Curzon and what was called "the Russianisation of the Indian Administration". Without sympathetic imagination no man could ever understand an alien people. Gokhale cited Gladstone's dictum, "it is liberty alone which fits men for liberty", against the counter doctrine, "wait till they are fit". He compared Curzon with Aurangzeb while others had produced the false parallel of Akbar. With Curzon as with Aurangzeb, "we find the same attempt at a rule excessively centralized and intensely personal, the same strenuous purpose, the same overpowering consciousness of duty, the same marvellous capacity for work, the same sense of loneliness, the same persistence in a policy of distrust and repression, resulting in bitter exasperation all round". And yet the Indian "extremists" hated Gokhale more than they hated even the British, just as the Mazzinians hated Cavour more even than they hated the Austrians.

In 1908 Aurobindo Ghosh had argued that the reason why even "a radical opportunist like Morley" refused Indians self-government was not that he did not believe in India's fitness for it but that he did not believe in India's determination to be free. Aurobindo attacked the "brief magic abracadabra of despotism", the semantics of imperialist self-justification which turned the peaceful acts of patriots into the illegitimate activities of criminals. He eschewed abstractions and formulas and spoke of practical necessities, the teaching of political experience, common sense and the world's history. Further, he said: "We recognize no political object of worship except the divinity in our Motherland, no present object of political endeavour except liberty, and no method or action as politically good or evil except as it truly helps or hinders our progress towards national emancipation." His attitude to bureaucratic concession was that of Laocoon: "We fear the Greeks even when they bring us gifts." In 1902 B.C. Pal spoke the language of Mazzini. India had its own special mission and its own peculiar destiny in the midst of humanity. "We desire to be in our own country as other peoples are in their country. We claim the right of controlling the course of historic evolution ourselves. We desire our own good and our own place in the universal scheme of things, and bear no ill-will towards any other people or country." Lala Lajpat Rai challenged the basis and sanction of the law under imperialist rule. "Only one feels disposed to smile when one hears of Indian nationalists being charged in British-Indian courts with attempting to subvert the government established by law. One is inclined to ask 'By what law'? and 'Who made that law'?" Rai felt that so long as there were Curzons, Macdonnels, and Sydenhams in the English Parliament, Indian Nationalism would not starve for want of congenial food. If British imperialists could sometimes be aroused to a sense of guilt, at least all patriots had to be aroused to a sense of shame at the affronts to their dignity and their cultural and political identity.

Among nationalists it was commoner to attack the imperialist system than to appeal to an individual sense of guilt. Gokhale declared: "It is the system which is really at fault – a system which relegates the interest of the people to a very subordinate place, and which, by putting too much power into the hands of these men, impairs their sense of responsibility and develops in them a spirit of intolerance of criticism." Surendranath Banerjea had said this as early as the seventh Congress: "it is not the men who are to blame; it is the system; it is the bureaucracy, the absolute despotism, that has been established, that must be arraigned before the bar of public opinion in India and throughout the civilized world". At the 29th Congress in 1914, Bhupendranath Basu warned that "the canonization of a bureaucracy" would mean perpetual tutelage; "an increasing dead weight on the soul of India, it would be a curse to civilization and a blot on humanity".

C. R. Das was scathing in his attack on "a system of benevolent despotism carried on through a self-willed bureaucracy." India no longer wanted trustees or guardians, utilitarian benefactors or evangelical soul-savers. Indian forbearance was strained to breaking-point. Despotism, however self-sacrificing and self-critical, was bound to be helpless and capricious, nervous and irresponsible. It was often inspired by panic because it could not be sure and was out of touch with public opinion. Indians would rather be governed by a cold, soulless, representative machinery than be fantastically treated to fits of concession and oppression by the best-meaning bureaucracy in the world. India had to develop a political personality of its own. "Without overrating itself, a people does not arrive at knowledge of itself at all." All government without the consent of the governed is, as Swift said, the very definition of slavery. In his presidential address to the Congress in 1922, C. R. Das challenged the whole political philosophy of the bureaucracy – the maintenance of law and order on the part of the government and an attitude of passive obedience and non-resistance on the part of the subject. "But was not that the political philosophy of every English king from William the Conqueror to James II? And was not that the political philosophy of the Romanoffs, the Hohenzollerns and of the Bourbons? And yet freedom has come, where it has come, by disobedience of the very laws which were proclaimed in the name of the law and order. Where the Government is arbitrary and despotic and the fundamental rights of the people are not recognized, it is idle to talk of law and order."

It was Gandhi's unique merit that in his combination of different methods, in his appeal to the British conscience, in his criticisms of the political theory of British imperialism, in his declaration of no confidence in the system, he was able to get down to fundamentals. He spoke in terms of Indian thought in accents of ringing sincerity and the deepest integrity that revealed courage, compassion, a patience born of strength and a purity that came through suffering. "An Englishman", he told C. F. Andrews, "never respects you till you stand up to him. Then he begins to like you. He is afraid of nothing physical; but he is very mortally afraid of his own conscience if ever you appeal to it, and show him to be in the wrong. He does not like to be rebuked for wrong-doing at first; but he will think it over, and it will get hold of him and hurt him till he does something to put it right." Gandhi did not directly appeal to British qualities of fair-play and justice; he took these for granted and went straight to the point. While his imperial antagonists preached Christianity and his Indian critics talked Hinduism, he practised both and thus confounded those who thought they could unnerve or undermine him. Similarly, he put his finger on the central assumptions of the four doctrines.

Only individuals could be trustees, not nations. No man loses his freedom except through his own weakness. A despotic government is maintained by the passive acquiescence of the people, by a hypnotic spell that has to be stoutly resisted. "Even the most despotic government cannot stand except for the consent of the governed which consent is often forcibly procured by the despot. Immediately the subject ceases to fear the despotic force, his power is gone." "The state represents violence in a concentrated and organized form. The individual has a soul, but as the state is a soulless machine, it can never be weaned from violence to which it owes its very existence." A votary of non-violence cannot subscribe to the utilitarian formula. "He will strive for the greatest good of all and die in the attempt to realize the ideal. . . . The greatest good of all inevitably includes the good of the greatest number, and therefore, he and the utilitarian will converge in many points of their career but there does come a time when they must part company, and even work in opposite directions. The utilitarian to be logical will never sacrifice himself. The absolutist will even sacrifice himself." As to guardianship, "there is no room for patronage among equals" and "there will never be equality so long as one feels inferior or superior to the other". Imperial domination must be replaced by a partnership on equal terms, a partnership that should not be 'subjection' in glorified language, like a relationship between a giant and a dwarf that was utilized for the exploitation of the other races of the earth. The British Empire, felt Gandhi, was an empire only because of India. A new concept of Indo-British partnership must emerge, "giving the promise of a world set free from exploitation". Every country was entitled to freedom without any question of its fitness or otherwise. "The doctrine of fitness to govern is a mere eyewash. Independence means nothing more or less than getting out of alien control." Real partnership must be "no cloak for rulership."

As to evangelical Christians, the least Gandhi could say was to doubt if they had benefited India and the most he could say was that "they have repelled India from Christianity and placed a barrier between Christian life and Hindu or Musalman life. When I go to your scriptures I do not see the barrier raised, but when I see a missionary I find that barrier rising up before my eyes. I want you to accept this testimony from one who was for a time susceptible to those influences . . . I have a definite feeling that if you want us to feel the aroma of Christianity, you must copy the rose. The rose irresistibly draws people to itself, and the scent remains with them. Even so, the aroma of Christianity is subtler even than the rose and should, therefore, be imparted in an even quieter, and more imperceptible manner, if possible." Further, the Christian imperialists had much to learn from Indian religious thought and ethics. No one chained a slave without chaining himself. And no nation kept another in subjection without itself turning into a subject nation. Imperialism was resulting in the 'brutalization of human beings'. "I know that people who voluntarily undergo a course of suffering raise themselves and the whole of humanity, but I also know that people who become brutalized in their desperate efforts to get victory over their opponents or to exploit weaker nations or weaker men not only drag down themselves but mankind also. And it cannot be a matter of pleasure to me or anyone else to see human nature dragged in the mire. If we are all sons of the same God and partake of the same divine essence, we must partake of the sin of every person whether he belongs to us or to another race."

To deny a nation its freedom was not to withhold a gift, but to deprive it of its birthright. Indians, too, had to suffer and sacrifice themselves in the attempt to gain their liberty. The aim must be a "partnership between two races, the one having been known for its manliness, bravery, courage and its unrivalled power of organization, and the other an ancient race possessing a culture perhaps second to none, a continent in itself". Such a partnership, as that between the Romans and the Greeks "cannot but result in mutual good and be to the benefit of mankind". Gandhi appealed to a gathering of Etonians not to follow slavishly, when they grew up, the footsteps of earlier empire builders like Wellesley, Metcalfe, Canning, Elgin, Dufferin, Lansdowne, Curzon and Irwin and many others, but instead "to make a unique contribution to the glory of your nation, by emancipating it from its sin of exploitation, and thus contribute to the progress of mankind".

He told a group of Oxford dons: "The long and short of it is that you will not trust us. Well, give us the liberty to make mistakes. If we cannot handle our affairs today, who is to say when we will be able to do so? I do not want you to determine the pace. Consciously or unconsciously you adopt the role of divinity. I ask you for a moment to come down from that pedestal. Trust us to ourselves, I cannot imagine anything worse happening than is happening today, a whole humanity lying prostrate at the feet of a small nation." At a much wider gathering in London, Gandhi asked, "Who is it that can say that you have conferred benefits on India? We or you? . . . A series of men, Naoroji, Pherozeshah Mehta, Ranade, Gokhale – who used to dote on you, who were proud of British contact and of the benefits conferred by your civilization – do you know that they are all agreed in saying that you have on the whole done harm to India? When you go, you will have left us an impoverished and emasculated people, and the shades of all who loved you will ask, what have you done during these years of tutelage? You must realize that we cannot afford to have doorkeepers at your rate of wages, for you are no better than doorkeepers and a nation with an income of two pence a day per head cannot pay those wages. . . . Well, was it not Sir Henry Campbell Bannerman who said that good government is no substitute for self-government? You, who are past masters in making mistakes, you, who in the language of Lord Salisbury know the art of blundering through to success, will you not give us the liberty of making mistakes? . . . The iron has entered the soul of thousands of men and women who are impatient of alien control. We are impatient to gain this freedom, with your help, if you will, without your help if we must."

Gandhi challenged all the assumptions underlying trusteeship, guardianship, utilitarianism and evangelicalism. He also stressed that the British imperialists were not bad but the victims of an evil system, "so that the system must be destroyed and not the individual". He believed in the English despite the system, not because of it. "I believe in the good faith of England to the extent that I believe in the good faith of human nature. I believe that the sum total of the energy of mankind is not to bring us down but to lift us up, and that is the result of the definite, if unconscious, working of the law of love." To Gandhi "we are all tarred with the same brush; we are all members of the vast human family. I decline to draw any distinctions. I cannot claim any superiority for Indians. We have the same virtues and the same vices."

Gandhi was able to appeal to the British sense of guilt as well as the Indian sense of shame rather than to British or Indian pride. He challenged British imperialism not on utilitarian but on moral grounds. To him the system was *Adharma*, devoid of any principle of moral authority or justification. The basic weakness of utilitarianism, in his eyes, was that is seemed to be a glorified power doctrine founded on a subtle form of violence. By talking the language of results, it led to a carelessness of the means, even an indifference to them. It could be invoked against notions of natural law and natural rights because it lent to factual considerations the emotive force of cherished values and matters of principle. Gandhi in his *Hind Swaraj* adopted a standpoint in regard to utilitarianism which was taken, to a lesser extreme, by Keynes in *Two Memoirs*. Keynes regarded it as "the worm which has been gnawing at the insides of modern civilization and is responsible for its present moral decay. We used to regard the Christians as the enemy, because they appeared as the representatives of tradition, convention, and hocus-pocus. In truth it was the Benthamite calculus, based on over-valuation of the economic criterion, which was destroying the quality of the popular Ideal." The final *reductio ad absurdum* of Benthamism was Marxism, a brutal and illegitimate descendant of the early proponents of state philanthropy and state patronage.

Benthamites and Marxists could employ their brands of utilitarianism to sanctify different forms of imperialism, as they could also be used in support of various types of nationalism. Just as Whiggery started back in horror at its spiritual offspring when it became the official creed of the revolted American colonies, so too imperialists recoil with shock when they find that their former theories are mirrored in the policies and doctrines of triumphant nationalists. The new ruling class in the Indian subcontinent achieves its ends by a utilitarian appeal to results. The leaders of the national movement, now in power, regard themselves as the natural trustees of popular welfare and behave at times like Platonic guardians of the masses in need of guidance. The religious evangelicalism of the past is now paralleled by a secular gospel of liberal, democratic socialism or by more unfamiliar and hybrid creeds. The role of trustees and of guardians and of missionaries is attractive to every *élite* in power, to every ruling class under modern representative government as under authoritarian régimes. How to justify the acquisition and the possession of power and what to do with power when justified are the problems that face every new government in the presence of an alert and vocal electorate or even of an acquiescent but potentially restless population. It is a great tribute to the methods and ideas of Gandhi that although he would not have approved of all the policies and doctrines of the new ruling class in India, it is possible to appeal to its sense of guilt as well as of shame, of betrayal as well as of failure when worthy ends are pursued by questionable methods or when worthy means are employed to achieve doubtful ends. This is especially valuable in the face of the authoritarian utilitarianism of ruthless Benthamite planners or Marxist dogmatists as well as the sectarian demands of religious fanatics.

It would be misleading to regard the political doctrines of British imperialism and especially of Benthamite utilitarianism as the direct cause of the political doctrines of Indian nationalism or of the present Indian government. Elements of trusteeship, guardianship, utilitarianism and even of missionary zeal can all be found in Indian political thought and tradition, although there are other and more dominant elements in Indian as in British thought and life. Behind all the failures and successes of the political theories of British imperialism lay the fact that the system they justified was a despotism and that the men who administered it were alien. Had the British settled down in the country and played the part of the Manchus in China, many of their theories and doings would have lasted longer and taken deeper root in Indian life, with the Indian genius for assimilation. Foreign rule could not be a proper, let alone a permanent, cure for the varied ills of Indian society that alone made foreign rule possible. The last thing that the imperialists thought of doing was to stimulate the growth of an organic political structure or a system of political ideas congenial to the new renaissance of ancient Indian civilization. Further, no material benefits, no cultural influences could outweigh the wrong of a relationship that lamed a people's will, insulted its self-respect and doomed it to passivity and political slavery. And yet, it was Indian weakness, not English strength that made English paramountcy possible. That the English solution to the problem of imperial government was worse than any alternative solution available to them in the context of their ideas or of the circumstances is not certain. It was in any case inevitable that, in Chinese terms, the mandate of Heaven would be withdrawn when it was challenged, and not the least proof of that inevitability was the persisting doubts and the strains of scepticism of the English about their imperial mission in India. Meanwhile, the imperialists had unwittingly brought into Indian society a new vitality and strength lacking in Moghul India, had unintentionally initiated the vigorous political awakening of the masses and the emergence of a new middle class which has been compared to the Roman equestrian order, "with the means and the will to check the power of the government". By the very application of their doctrines, the trustees, the guardians, the utilitarians and the evangelicals brought about their own downfall, leaving behind them scattered traces of their thought and vocabulary.

# THE 1958 REVOLUTION IN PAKISTAN

*By Guy Wint*

THE REVOLUTION IN Pakistan which happened in October 1958 was the overthrow of the Western style of parliamentary democracy. It was a political and not a social or cultural revolution. It was not the overthrow of the liberal system of society. The new régime has declared itself anxious to preserve this, and its actions, at least up to the present, show that it is sincere.

The military *coup* in Pakistan was the most striking of a recent series of revolutions in Asia and Africa in which the army has displaced civilian rule. Pakistan is by far the largest of the countries in which this has happened, and thus makes the most striking case-study. Moreover, as Pakistan is within the Commonwealth, and the Commonwealth has had for the first time to accommodate a military dictatorship, its vicissitudes started more reflections in England than had been roused by other countries which had had rather similar experiences. The problem facing the spectator is whether the military *coups* show a general trend, in Asia and among the new states generally, towards a new and military form of government. Is military rule likely to be stable, and does it represent a third possible pattern for the future besides Communism and parliamentary democracy?

The inquiries about Pakistan have been made under a handicap because since 1947 the British people have grown out of touch with the country. No British newspaper has kept a full-time correspondent at Karachi.

I spent March and April of 1959 in Pakistan. The new régime had been in existence for about half a year, and had attained a certain stability. What follows is some notes on how Pakistan appeared to a visitor at that time, and what are its prospects.

*Why the Revolution Happened*

After independence, Pakistan adopted a system of parliamentary government very similar to that of India. But its experience in working it was less impressive. It took many years in drafting its permanent constitution. The constituent assembly was formed out of the Moslem members of parliament from the former Indian legislature. Many of these came from the United Provinces and Bihar, and saw little prospect of being elected for a Pakistan constituency. Their interest lay therefore in spinning out the proceedings of the constituent assembly. While it was sitting, they could enjoy all the perquisites. Its dissolution meant their end.

Thus it was not until 1955 that the constitution was completed. Pakistan never experienced a general election, unlike India, which has held two nation-wide general elections in the years since independence. Few experiences are so politically educative, or bring a country along so fast, as a general election.

The causes of the failure of Pakistan democracy go deeper than this. The chief among them was the weakness of the party system; and here again the contrast is striking. Unlike India, Pakistan did not have to struggle for a long time for its freedom. The ease with which it was obtained exacted a heavy price later.

India fought for freedom for forty years. The long struggle caused the Indian National Congress to develop as a cohesive well-organised party which preserved its own inner discipline fairly well. The national struggle tempered it. The internal democracy of the Congress Party, by which office holders had constantly to offer themselves to the party for re-election, strengthened the habit of acting through democratic processes.

In Pakistan there had been no such preparation for self-government. Independence was given to Pakistan: it was not struggled for. True, the Moslem League acted in the last years of the British Raj as the spear-head for the demand for the creation of Pakistan. But the Moslem League never had to fight, except for a few weeks at the end of the British Raj against the Unionist Government in the Punjab, and this was not a very formidable antagonist. As a result, parties had never become really rooted in the masses.

Another reason why the parliamentary system failed in Pakistan was that at independence Pakistan had a very weak middle class; and the parliamentary system works best where there is a large and strong middle class. Indeed, parliamentary democracy seems really to have been devised by the middle class for the middle class. Such middle class as existed in Pakistan had been largely Sikh and Hindu; and, at the partition in West Pakistan, all but the Moslems decamped. In East Pakistan the Hindu middle class tried at first to remain, but became the target of a social revolution which sought to deprive it of its privileges. It could not give political leadership.

Where a parliamentary system functions well, it is usually as the political expression of a complex society in which public debate is carried on the whole time, and by a great many different means – in the press, in private discussion, in universities, among the trade unions, in the clash of societies and pressure groups. Often the public opinion of the country is formed in this way before an issue comes before parliament, and parliament merely ratifies what has been already decided on. No such system existed in Pakistan. The society of Pakistan was simple, not complex. Parliamentary institutions existed against a void background.

Power in Pakistan was a monopoly of fifty or a hundred families. In the days after independence they laid their hands on the key positions of authority. Their success was easier because of the extinction of the Hindus and Sikhs in West Pakistan, and their demotion in East Pakistan. These families supplied the members of parliament, the bureaucracy, owned the newspapers, owned the land, dominated industry and commerce, and also ran the opposition.

In this environment, parliament functioned. The political parties were not solid organisations, and they were not under strong pressure from public opinion. They did not represent great organised interests. They were shifting combinations of members of the parliamentary assemblies – rather like the parties in 18th-century England. To a great extent they were the personal following of large landowners, who marshalled their tenants to vote as they directed. The parties were volatile kaleidoscopes. The governments which held office by grace of these parties were liable to be overthrown with every change in the kaleidoscope. In latter years, each cabinet lasted only a few months.

The trouble was increased because there was no tradition of parliamentary government in Pakistan. Parliament in British days had not acclimatised itself in the Moslem parts of India as strikingly as it did in the Hindu parts. True, parliament was regarded as an attractive centre for obtaining jobs and influence. But the instinctive practices, habits of mind, and connections which made parliamentary government easy to operate had never grown up. The Islamic tradition was one of autocracy, tempered by sagacious counsellors.

One trouble was that the parliaments in Pakistan did not throw up any born parliamentary statesmen – men who, however autocratic by nature, turned by habit to parliament, as in England men like Winston Churchill have done. Jinnah himself, though a good debater, was far too dictatorial by temperament. Liaquat Ali Khan was nearest to being a good parliamentary leader. After him, nobody imposed his personality on the parliaments, elevated their proceedings, guided their development.

The failure of the parliamentary system in Pakistan was the sadder because in one respect Pakistan had begun with an advantage not enjoyed by other countries. Except in East Bengal, society was not divided into a permanent majority and a permanent minority. It is this division which has brought parliament to ruin in so many countries. The parliamentary system can work well only when the minority of today can look forward to being the majority of tomorrow. Where this does not happen, the minority looks to other means to protect its interests. But grievances of this kind played no part in the military *coup*. The Hindu minority in East Bengal had no share in bringing it about.

One result of the defective parliamentary system was that the Governor-General began to play a part in politics never intended for him by the constitution. After the departure of Nizam-ud-din, Pakistan never enjoyed the possession of a weak, a figure-head Governor-General, such as parliamentary politics require. The Governor-General's palace was occupied by strong and restless men (one of them a chronic invalid, but nevertheless a match for the whole of the rest of the political system). They itched to intervene, and they did intervene; and they devised the methods for their intervention as they went along. Ghulam Mohammed and Iskander Mirza were successively the real rulers of the country. They overshadowed their prime ministers, dismissed them as they chose (with doubtful constitutional propriety, but nobody protested effectively), played off the politicians against one another, ran political parties in their own interest, and centred the entire political life of the country increasingly on the presidential palace.

The result of all these factors was that Pakistan had a deplorably bad system of government. It failed to make the reforms which the society demanded if it was to progress, such as the land reform; it failed to fulfil its urgent immediate obligations, such as the settlement of refugees;

it failed to improve agricultural production or increase the literacy rate; it failed even to design a capital city appropriate to a country of eighty million people. Under the government there grew up a belief that everything was for sale. The clever crook was able to thrive. Law was not enforced against the well-to-do. Taxes were evaded. The operators of smuggling gangs had many of the key figures in administration in their pay. Prices rose continually.

It is true that in retrospect the parliamentary régime may have been blackened too much. Its defects, gross as they were, may have been magnified. The extent of corruption is quickly exaggerated as the stories about it are passed from mouth to mouth. Yet there can be no doubt that the faults of the régime were excessive.

The government and politicians were despised. In contrast, the army gained prestige. For the army was both conspicuously efficient and conspicuously incorrupt. It was a small army – no larger than eight divisions – and this had helped in maintaining its morale. It was tightly knit and well disciplined. It took pride in maintaining the traditions derived from the British army. It was competent because it lived by a time-table, and nobody else in Pakistan dreamed of doing so.

Thus an unbalance developed between the respected and capable army, and the despised and incompetent politicians. The army might have moved into political control earlier but for one thing: its commanders had taken over the British tradition that an army should keep aloof from politics. They had twice refused invitations to set up a dictatorship by the former Governor-General Ghulam Mohammed. In the end their scruples were overcome.

The signal for action was an incident in East Bengal. A general election had been scheduled for February 1959. It was taken for granted that the parties in power at the time would win the elections because they could rig them. Thus the struggle to keep, or gain, power rose to a new crescendo. As part of the manœuvre the opposition in the East Bengal parliament had managed to get the Speaker certified as mad, and had replaced him by the deputy speaker, who was one of the opposition's sympathisers. The supporters of the government did not take this lying down. At the next session of the parliament they brought in planks of wood and threw them at the deputy speaker. One of them hit him, and he died. This gave the army its cue for action.

One result of these discreditable happenings was that none of the politicians whom the army deposed was able to make a protest. They simply withdrew. There was no fight in them, and the reason was that they knew they could raise almost no public support if they opposed the army. After the first few days, public opinion supported the revolution. Only one speech against the dictatorship was made, and that not by a politician but by the Chief Justice of West Pakistan. Some of the politicians doubtless hoped that time would bring new changes, and with them their eventual reinstatement. Others hoped that the new régime might employ them as ambassadors, or allow them the foreign exchange to travel abroad. Quietness and acquiescence seemed to be the only way.

### *First Days of the New Régime*

For the first few days the army was rough. It set up martial law courts. Under martial law regulations these could deal with cases of black-marketing, smuggling, and tax evasion. They handed out some rather savage sentences. But only in one case does the sentence seem to have been monstrous – seven years for a young reporter for heckling a general at a press conference. Even at their roughest, the martial law courts were not wild. They acted judicially: counsel could appear before them. A High Court judge remarked that he had more confidence in some of them than in some subordinate civilian courts.

This phase was soon over. The army foray into the ordinary administration lasted only a few days. General Ayub, the Commander-in-Chief – now President – who had made the revolution, had no intention of letting the army get bogged down in politics. It was ordered back to its professional duties. Ayub claimed that even though the army had to carry out the revolution it did not lose a single day of its professional training.

Afterwards, the country was ruled by a cabinet at the centre, and by the civil service. The cabinet consisted of three generals (one of them a medical man) and eight civilians. The outstanding civilian figure was the Foreign Minister, Manzur Qadir, a well-known Lahore lawyer. The cabinet ran the country through the civil service. Thus the system was rather like the British Raj in its most authoritarian days, before constitutions were thought of. The difference was that the régime was an interim one. A new basis would have to be found. Moreover there was not, as in the days of the British Raj, a parliamentary public opinion at Westminster which in the last resort would control the government.

There was the added difficulty that the civil service had become corrupt during the parliamentary period. Too many burdens and also temptations had been placed upon it. It had been too small at its start. Of the former administrative service, the Indian Civil Service, only about fifty members had opted for service in Pakistan. This was not enough to transmit a tradition. The service in its new shape was not able to remain spotless when under pressure from ministers or when confronted with opportunities for illicit enrichment. The corruption became common knowledge.

The army was more indignant against the civil service than against the politicians. It argued that politicians were past praying for, but the civil service should have known better. Nevertheless the army could not do without the civil service. Even though it proclaimed itself the champion of the State against corruption, it could not afford to proceed against all the corrupt members of the civil service, because if it had done so it would have been left without a machine to govern the country. It comprised by submitting all civil servants to a screening and an analysis of their private wealth. As a result, about eighty members, at all levels, were dismissed, and the army trusted that the example of their fate would cause the remainder to reform themselves.

The government had taken dictatorial powers, but in most cases the taking of the powers was enough: it did not have to use them. After the first days of the régime very few persons were kept under arrest without trial: in West Pakistan in April 1959 the number was down to nine. Martial law regulations gave the government sweeping powers over the press, but most newspapers were so ready to collaborate with the government that there was no need for repression. The most high-handed act by government was to put new managers in charge of the country's best-edited newspaper, the *Pakistan Times*; it intervened there because the *Pakistan Times* received subsidies by ingenious means from China and Czechoslovakia. There was no terror by a secret police. The army was hardly visible at all. Soldiers are more in evidence in London than they were in Karachi or Lahore.

### *The Government's Record*

The achievements during the first months of the military government – or semi-military government – were real. It had more beneficient action to its credit than any previous government in Pakistan. Its first actions were to try to check the price rise. The methods were crude, but they brought many prices down by as much as 40%. This could not be lasting. Some goods disappeared from the markets, and prices rose again. Nevertheless, the price fixing gave the government its popularity in the first days after the revolution.

The government has to be assessed by its longer-range programme. It promulgated land reform in the western half of the federation. This was one of the crying needs of the country. In the Punjab and Sindh there are huge landed estates – in the Punjab at least one of 200,000 acres. The landlords dominated the parliamentary elections. This was one reason why a modern party system could not develop: there were too many pocket boroughs. Feeling in favour of a land reform had been growing. The civil service regarded it as necessary, so did the business class, which saw in the feudal organisation of the countryside an obstacle to the economic development of the country. But under the parliamentary system every plan for reform had been blocked in the legislatures or sabotaged in implementation.

By the measure decree in February 1959 a landlord might not retain more than 500 acres of irrigated land or 1,000 acres of dry land. (He could keep 150 acres of orchard in addition to this.) The rest of his estates was to be taken by the Government and redistributed. The landlord was to receive compensation in bonds at perhaps a quarter of the market value. The ceiling is well above the holding of most officers in the army, and thus the measure did not offend the army, even though the army represents agrarian interests. In other ways also the measure was less drastic than appeared at first sight. Five hundred acres of irrigated land may give a very large income. Moreover, most landlords as a precaution have distributed their holdings fairly widely among their relations, while keeping control of them by behind-the-scenes methods. In spite of this the measure really was radical, though Left-Wing critics tried to denigrate it. Its effect was to deflate the political predominance of the landlords. The measure was a precedent. More radical land reform would be easier to introduce.

The scheme was prepared quickly, but, in contrast with the Indian plan for cooperative farming, was not slipshod or badly thought out. It was drawn up by an expert commission of enquiry. This was the working method which Ayub had developed when he was Commander-in-Chief. When he is faced with a problem, he sets up an expert commission to find a solution, and once it has reported he implements the solution rapidly. In the present case there were only five days between the commission making its report and the government declaring its policy. The scheme was translated into martial law regulations. The purpose was to ensure that the implementation would not be held up, as had happened in India, by appeals to the ordinary courts with all their cumbersome procedure.

Another constructive achievement was the settlement of the urban refugees. Nearly two million urban refugees from India had been living a hand-to-mouth existence. Their plight had for a long while been a scandal, but none of the many governments had done anything for them. They lived in a kind of improvised kennels, and governments were so shameless about their neglect that they allowed them on the very route from the military airfield taken by V.I.P. visitors to Karachi. One of the generals in the new cabinet, Azam Khan, was given responsibility for them. He dealt with the problem in the spirit of a general clearing up a bad state of affairs in a cantonment. A rapid survey was made of their condition. The government used students of Karachi university as fact-finders. Their reports were collated and published in record time. They were almost unbelievably shocking to read.

Action followed. The government, helped by the Ford Foundation, engaged the Greek consultant Doxiades, and hustled the construction of a satellite town near Karachi at a place called Korangi. The first refugees began to move in in July. The new houses were not luxurious, but they were water-tight and they had sanitation and running water. Employment and transportation were provided. By the end of the year, 100,000 refugees had been housed, and there are plans, well advanced, for seven other towns.

By action of this kind the government convinced enlightened opinion that it really had a programme. Other commissions were set up, with instructions to draw up plans for further reform – on education, on the press, on whether the capital should be moved from Karachi, on the reorganisation of the law courts and of regional administration. They were given a zero hour by which to report. The commission on the capital recommended its eventual transfer to a new site near Rawalpindi.

### *Back to a Constitution*

The new régime, however, good its record, was not meant to continue indefinitely. From the earliest days of the revolution President

Ayub insisted that the system was only temporary. He admitted that it had no basis in legality, and reposed simply on force, and, though this might be permissible over the short run, he did not regard it as a tolerable permanent solution. Permanent military dictatorship was not thought of. It was taken for granted that there must be a return to legality and to constitutional government. The search for the way back began within a month or two of the *coup*.

An axiom was that the next constitution could not be like the one abrogated by the army in October 1958. What would be the point of bringing back that, asked Ayub? It would merely restore the politicians and the system which had brought the country to disaster. The diagnosis of Ayub and his colleagues was that that constitution had been defective because it provided for a cabinet which could be overturned at will by the legislature. They wanted instead an executive which would be elected but which, once elected, would have a continuity of tenure. This drove them towards the idea of an American or presidential form of democracy.

This idea did not commend itself very favourably to the country's intelligentsia. Their attachment to British forms of government is remarkably strong; they did not like forsaking them for American forms. Yet the facts of the situation were on Ayub's side.

The new ideas took shape gradually, in consultation between Ayub, Manzur Qadir, and some other senior colleagues. They planned to make the President not only the titular head of state but also the chief executive. He would be elected, but elected indirectly. Ayub and his advisers mistrusted the capacity of the mass of the people to act politically. They argued that the villager – who forms the largest part of the electorate – is better able to select one good man to act and speak for him than to discriminate between political leaders whom he does not know. Basing themselves on this, they devised a plan of organising the electorate into units of a thousand; each of these units was to select one candidate who would then form part of an electoral college to vote for the President. The voting age would be 25, and there would be no property qualification.

This plan came under a good deal of criticism. It was pointed out that it is cheaper for corrupt politicians to corrupt a small electoral college than an entire electorate.

Once an executive could be elected for a fixed term, Ayub and his advisers saw no objection to the return of the political parties. They saw the function of parties as being in legislatures which could legislate, criticise, question – but not overturn the government. These legislatures could be freely elected. But some of the more discreditable politicians of the past might be barred from further activity.

Further progress with the plan was made at a conference of officials at Natiagali in June. It was announced that assemblies or *panchayets* would be set up in four tiers – starting with the village *panchayet* at the lowest, and rising to an assembly at the level of the commissioners division.

The first stage of the programme was put into operation at the mid-winter of 1959–60. Eight thousand village councils were elected by popular vote. The 80,000 elected members were then formed into an electoral college to give a vote confirming Ayub Khan as national president. Next, a small constitution commission was to be set up, handpicked by government; and its task will be to produce a draft of the constitution, which will then be submitted to a plebiscite – or, alternatively, will be voted on by an electoral college produced by indirect election. Ayub argued that experience had shown the uselessness of entrusting constitution-making to a large elected body. It would take years to finish its work.

One of Ayub's main concepts was that if his work was to succeed, the revolution must remain bloodless. He was fully aware of the passionate forces in Pakistan's political life. Once shooting started, passion would take control. Ayub quoted Winston Churchill: "The grass grows quickly over the battlefield. Over the scaffold, never."

There are few instances in history where an army, after once taking power, hands it back voluntarily to civilian hands. Ayub seemed genuinely bent on doing this, after the army revolution had finished its work of purification. The reason he gave was that politics is a dirty business – and if the army stayed in it too long it would itself be corrupted.

### *A Young Officer's Revolution*

Obviously a government behaving so mildly and moderately deserved credit and support. But it was precarious. The means used by Ayub for taking power could be used by other people – say young officers – for taking power from him.

Soon after the new régime was established, the spectre of a young officer's revolution began to haunt many visitors to Karachi. If it had come about, some foreigners would have done a good deal to promote it. They talked about it so much – especially Indians and Americans – that they might have ended by putting ambitions into the minds of young officers which they would otherwise not have entertained.

Of course, the danger was real enough. Memory was still fresh about the Rawalpindi conspiracy case in 1952 when the then Chief of Staff and a group of officers were arrested for plotting to seize power, and were imprisoned.

Personal contact with the Pakistani army reduced some of the anxiety. The Pakistani army was extremely impressive. It was a thoroughly professional army. It prided itself on taking over the British tradition of the army's aloofness from day-to-day politics. Officers were discouraged from talking politics in their Mess. They were shocked at the suggestion that they might behave like a Middle East army.

Ayub was confident that he could keep in check any misplaced radicalism in the army. He knew the army through and through. Probably his confidence was well placed. But it was hard for an outsider to be sure. After all, who can have been more confident about the loyalty of their subordinate officers than the commanders of the Indian army in the first days of 1857, a month or so before the Mutiny?

The test of Ayub's authority may come when he is getting ready to restore a constitutional form of government. If the reckless young men really exist, they might decide that that was the time to strike. The army is conscious of its superior efficiency and superior honesty. This constitutes a temptation to keep power in its hands.

*Prospects*

The régime had to pay special regard to two dangerous possibilities. One was the disruption of the Pakistani state, and an attempted secession by East Bengal.

Friction between East and West Pakistan had existed ever since Pakistan was founded. The two halves of the country spoke different languages; ethnographically the peoples differed. There were economic and political grievances. If by the letter of the constitution East Pakistan was given equality in the State, there was a lively feeling that the letter was evaded. East Pakistan earned two-thirds of the country's foreign exchange and complained that the West took the benefits.

The fear after the *coup* was that the grievances might grow stronger because East Pakistan would regard army rule as alien rule. The army officers consisted chiefly of Pathans and Punjabis: only 5% were Bengalis. The average army officer was ignorant about the Bengali outlook. One general was heard to remark: "Of course we know more about London than we know about Dacca." East Pakistan was much more political than West: the political parties were more active, the people had a talent for political action. They would chafe more quickly than the Westerners at a continuing prohibition of political life.

All this was true. Yet secession was unlikely. East Pakistan had celebrated its separation from India by driving out a part of its Hindu minority, especially the part which enjoyed privilege or was economically powerful. It feared the return of this Hindu ascendancy, and it knew that this would be the result if it seceded from West Pakistan and rejoined India. Therefore, though it would grumble, it was unlikely to do more.

The second danger was Communism. For the time being it was not a very imminent danger. The Communist Party had been proscribed for several years before the army *coup*. Where a Communist movement has not already got off the ground, it is relatively easy to keep it throttled by such means. In West Pakistan the clandestine organisation was totally ineffective. In the East, there was a more serious underground movement which operated from Indian soil at Calcutta.

Communism might spread rapidly if President Ayub delayed too long in bringing in a new constitution, and in legitimising the political parties. For where no parties are allowed, one party always thrives – the Communist Party. People join it, not because they want Communism, but because it seems to be the only determined political organisation. Another danger was of an intensified Communist campaign of subversion from Indian territory. This might happen if the Indian state of West Bengal went Communist at a general election.

One result of the revolution was to open up quite new possibilities in the political development of Pakistan. Before the revolution, the political leaders invariably lent a polite ear to projects of wide-visioned reform or political construction, but invariably replied that they could do nothing: it was not practical politics: the votes could not be gathered. After the revolution, votes, at least for the time, did not matter. There was a new elasticity in the matters which the new régime was willing to discuss. Revolution had brought political open-mindedness.

*Conclusion*

The art of Ayub's government was to equip itself with dictatorial powers – and then not to use them. It calculated that because these powers remained in the background, the enemies of the régime would not risk opposition. Out of prudence, the opposition would not harry the government.

Whether the calculation was sound depended on whether the army could retain its prestige. That was the uncertain factor. In the first months of the new régime, most of the intellectuals and progressives supported it, even if ruefully, because it meant sound administration, and because there was no alternative. But how would the army be regarded a year or two later if it had not by then restored representative institutions, and if economic grievances had been multiplied?

The essential nature of the Pakistani revolution is that it was a political revolution, whose purpose was to find new institutions of government which would administer the country more effectively. But the social system which it was to administer was to go on unchanged. This was what, broadly speaking, can be called the liberal society; it meant the rule of law, the freedom of the individual, the freedom of the judiciary from the executive, the rights of free thought and free speech, the existence (within limits) of free newspapers. All these things are still valued in Pakistan. Paradoxically, the public seems to feel that they are safer under the military, at least under the generals who now hold ultimate power, than they were under the politicians. Pakistan has not turned its back on what it acquired from Britain.

The nature of the Pakistani army is so peculiar to the country, the personality of General Ayub so exceptional, that Pakistan's example may not be very significant for other countries. Other countries may suffer the same misgovernment as Pakistan under its parliamentary régime. But they cannot rely on the military remedies producing the same efficient and moderate results.

# THE SOVIET RE-ASSESSMENT OF MAHATMA GANDHI

*By Kyril Tidmarsh*

SHORTLY AFTER THE death of Tolstoy, Lenin attacked the "venal hacks" of Tsarist historiography who "yesterday had been ordered to hound Lev Tolstoy and today to show that Tolstoy is a patriot and to observe the rules of convention before Europe". Of the press which was capable of such a change of face he wrote that "it is replete to nausea with hypocrisy".[1] It is ironical, however, that in more recent times Soviet historians have been equally equivocal in their estimates of Tolstoy.

With Tolstoy we are not concerned in this paper, but, until the death of Stalin, the assessment by Soviet historians of Gandhi – whose name has always been closely linked with that of Tolstoy – was regrettably of a nature which is just as guilty of the Leninist charge of hypocrisy.

Two things strike one as one reads through the successive descriptions of Gandhi in the Soviet press. First of all, Gandhi for the Russians was never a man. His innate goodness as a human being, his self-sacrificial fasts, the way in which he applied to his personal life the tenets he advocated for others, his views on personal morality – all these are totally unknown to the Russian reader. For the Russians, Gandhi was depersonified. In the West – in the U.S.A. and Europe just as much as in this country – Gandhi has been a household word. Nurses the world over referred to their children as little Gandhis if they were inordinantly thin or under-dressed. In Russia this, at any rate, was inconceivable. The few references to Gandhi in the daily papers at the time of his great fasts, for instance – let alone in the more specialised periodical press – were invariably in the most abstract of terms. Throughout the various twists and turns of the Soviet interpretation of Gandhism, the figure of Gandhi himself has remained constant; abstract, disembodied, he was simply a lifeless symbol.

[1] V. I. Lenin, "Lev Tolstoy as a mirror of the Russian Revolution" in *Sochineniya* (4th edition), vol. XV, p. 179

Secondly, since Gandhi was never viewed as an individual, he was seen from a strictly Marxist point of view as representative of a class, and his every action was interpreted as a reflection of the views or aims of the Indian bourgeoisie. For this reason, the Soviet view of Gandhi throughout the period since the Revolution – which covers the main span of Gandhi's activity in India after his return from South Africa – is of particular interest to the student of international affairs. In the fluctuating attitude of the Soviet historian, in his every change of nuance, there is clearly reflected the changing Soviet attitude towards the colonial bourgeoisie and towards the appearance of a powerful new state on the borderland of the U.S.S.R.

Originally, in the early 20's, the Russians regarded the Indian National Congress as a kind of acceptable *faute de mieux*.

> Congress [wrote *Kommunisticheski Internatsional* in 1921] is slowly feeling its way towards popular trust, securing for itself strong support from the people for what is already announced as the next requirement of the programme – the mass refusal by the citizens to obey the government or to pay taxes. The formation of a central national organization which, in the eyes of the majority of the population without distinction of caste, creed or language, one should obey over the head of the British administration, is in itself no small accomplishment.[2]

Gandhi's policy is seen as the only one which was practicable at this time.

> At first glance, Gandhi appears as a demented prophet of non-violence and peace. But a close acquaintance with his teaching and his tactics convinces one that he consciously selected the only path open to Indian patriots under the present régime of oppression . . . under present circumstances there can be no question of an armed political revolt in India. For this reason, there remains only the one course – to attempt to unify the national consciousness by various other means until the day dawns when its power will be seen as irresistible. Gandhi himself had said at Lucknow: "Our duty is first of all to pursue our work in a *practical* direction; we cannot take to the sword – for it would not be within our strength to shatter the British Empire with the sword. Poor people, possessing no aeroplanes become willy-nilly supporters of the boycott and of other

[2] *Kommunisticheski Internatsional* (1921), p. 5067

means requiring no force, and there exists no other means for them."[3]

When the question was raised whether the boycott was equivalent to non-political 'bread-and-butter' strikes in the West and therefore harmful in that it diverted the attention of the working class away from the political struggle, the reply was evasive and the importance of Gandhism as a temporary measure, preparing the workers and peasants for the coming struggle, was stressed:

> We do not intend to inquire into the question how far the boycott can be justified from an economic point of view, for it is based primarily upon emotional factors whose success can be impeded by a variety of questions. We are more interested in the wide perspectives – the undoubted existence in India of a widespread consciousness of national solidarity, a nationalistic exaltation and desire to finish with the existing government order – all this heralds an intensification of the struggle . . . if India, by one means or another, ceases to be of profit to England, then the British authority in the country will weaken and eventually disappear. There will be no need for England to hold the country by force, with the help of a policy contrary to the people's will. If England comes to find that the Indian empire brings it no benefit, it will allow the Indians to take their own path.[4]

Even the fundamental incompatibility with Marxism of Gandhi's objection to Western technology was brushed aside:

> Gandhi's call back to the spinning wheel has a direct and practical aim – whatever we might think of the economic impossibility of replacing by manual means the vast quantity of clothes hitherto imported. Indeed, at the present time, the Indian factories can manufacture only half the required quantity. However, just as the teaching of non-violence – independently of its ideological content – brought advantage in that it cleared the way for a nationwide propaganda which would inevitably hit out against governmental repressions, so too the thought at the basis of the boycott has a two-fold significance: on the one hand, it fosters local industry, hindering the import of foreign goods and, on the other hand, brings nationalist ideas among the masses and places upon them the accomplishment of

[3] *Kommunisticheski Internatsional* (1921), p. 5067 [4] *op. cit.*, p. 5073

practical aims so that, by means of a widespread propaganda among the people, it might further unify it for a more resolute striving towards the ultimate goal.[5]

From the religious point of view also, Gandhi was acceptable in that he brought Muslims and Hindus together on a national programme:

> The aim of Gandhi is to convince the Muslims to regard themselves, first and foremost, as Indians and to fight for the Caliphate on Indian territory.[6]

Over the next few years, the Soviet attitude to Gandhi began to undergo a complex change. There appear to have been two factors at work. First, the natural impact upon communist theoreticians of the events of 1921 leading up to Gandhi's important decision at Bardoli, which amounted to renunciation of any opposition which might end in violence and, in fact, the kind of struggle for which Marxists stood. Secondly, four years later, there was Stalin's pronouncement upon the subject. This was undoubtedly the decisive factor and set the pattern of official interpretation on all future Soviet judgements on Gandhi.

It is noteworthy that, at the time, the decision at Bardoli was not seen as "the great betrayal" which it became for Soviet historians at a later date. The main reason for this would appear to be that the significance of the decision was believed to amount to the political suicide of Gandhi. *Novy Vostok* wrote:

> This shows that the Congress movement has come into an *impasse*, that it is losing its authority. The first indication of the correctness of this is that the arrest and conviction of "saintly Gandhi" to a six year term of imprisonment, aroused no kind of reaction and went almost unnoticed among the masses.[7]

Until Stalin pronounced on the subject, references to the positive aspects of Gandhism were still in print:

> the movement of boycott had done its task and had brought positive gain to the aim of national struggle. It gave to the national movement a mass character and it was able to unite Muslims and Hindus in a demand for national independence for India. This was a very important accomplishment . . . By a clever tactical move, Congress seized this trump card from the British, including the demand for

[5] *op. cit.*, p. 5074 [6] *Ibid.* [7] *Novy Vostok* (1922), No. I, p. 115

a Caliphate in its programme. But the main accomplishment of Congress was that the clarion call to independence – which had been the heritage of the privileged classes of the bourgeoisie and intelligentsia – became active, massive and popular. This was achieved by Gandhi's tactic of boycott, which was acceptable and easily understandable by the widest masses.

Having accomplished this positive task, however, the episode of Gandhism in Indian history was regarded as closed. It had become anachronistic and new methods of struggle were expected to take the field:

> Gandhi's tactic has now been outdated [wrote *Novy Vostok*]. For the further leadership of the masses, there is need of new mottos and slogans – more topical, more active and closer to the people . . .
>
> Can the present leaders of Congress supply them?
>
> No.
>
> For this, they are too much permeated with the spirit of passive resistance – for this, they are too tied up with the direct interests of the bourgeoisie who fear a revolutionary explosion.[8]

The same was repeated by another Soviet commentator:

> Gandhi has ceased to play the role of being a positive factor on the stage of Indian national politics since the time of the contemptible decision at Bardoli. The followers of Gandhi who remained with him after his arrest still tried to uphold his misty-sublime programme against the criticism of bourgeois commonsense . . .[9]

But the back of Gandhism was broken.

> Who has remained with Gandhi? The large landowning and financial bourgeoisie had never been behind him. The native industrial bourgeoisie went over to Das. The radical intelligentsia found itself divided between two parties. Thus there remained behind Gandhi only the small bourgeoisie: shopkeepers, a few petty landowners and artisans – those layers of the Indian population whose ideology was directly attracted by the socially reactionary teaching of Gandhism. This strata, by its class nature and actual position in India, was incapable of any lengthy political struggle. When the

[8] *Novy Vostok* (1922), No. IX

[9] *Kommunisticheski Internatsional* (1925), No I, p. 133.

dust of the revolutionary years had settled, the shopkeepers and petty *zemindars* returned to their peaceful activity and refused to participate even in the harmless *hartals* from time to time still practised by Congress. Only by this complete desertion on the part of the nationalists who had followed the Mahatma can one explain that Gandhi, in spite of his aura of martyrdom and saintliness, suffered a serious defeat as soon as he left prison. Already at the June Plenum of the Central Committee of Congress when Gandhi tried to carry through a resolution excluding Swarajists from controlling positions, he suffered a shameful defeat. Gandhi himself clearly felt that the ground was slipping from beneath his feet.[10]

Gandhi's agreement with the Swarajists was seen as the complete capitulation of his movement. It is, however, significant that no ideological conclusion was drawn as yet from the Bardoli decision; it was only Stalin who was to discern its sinister implication. Das's Swaraj party which was seen to be replacing Gandhi's influence and which was admitted to be of more Right-Wing tendency was nevertheless still regarded as a progressive influence. The author of this article, Mr Freier, states that:

> Under this pressure (from the industrial bourgeoisie) Das's Party was turning increasingly to the right. Nevertheless, this party still remains a progressive factor in Indian national politics in that it represents the young progressive Indian bourgeoisie whose interests everywhere come into conflict with the interests of the imperialist bourgeoisie.[11]

In May 1925 – a mere month before Stalin's crucial speech – still another writer saw the only objection to the Congress Party and to Gandhism in their betrayal by Gandhi himself who deprived them of leadership. The doctrine, however, was still as acceptable as ever.

> It is ridiculous [writes the author of an article on "Class Differentiation in the Revolutionary Movement of India"] to place responsibility for defeat upon the programme when it was the leaders who had consciously sabotaged the movement . . . the programme of passive resistance was fully realistic and could be carried through to the enormous damage of British imperialism, had it not been for the deliberate sabotage by the leaders. It was to such an extent realistic –

[10] *Ibid.* [11] *Ibid.*

that is to say, it corresponded so well to the conditions in which the country found itself at that time – that even the half-hearted and cautious propaganda in favour of this programme brought the masses into a condition of revolutionary ferment. . . . The Gandhist leaders took fright at those forces which they had called into existence and gave the signal for a retreat, although all circumstances were favourable for energetic, aggressive measures. Up to now, all stages of the boycott were but preparatory steps for the most significant part of the programme – the refusal to pay taxes and the launching of a mass disobedience of the laws. The programme was fully realistic. It was at the same time a most revolutionary programme. Its aim was to give political expression to the displeasure of the mass. No better method existed for the destruction of the political and economic structure of imperialism. However, from the very beginning, the bourgeois leaders sought to avoid any step which would lead up to such a crisis. The nationalist movement in the post-war period took upon itself a popular character and it was quite impossible to throw out of the programme those slogans which represented the true demands of the people. When these demands were brought forward they were formulated in the vaguest of terms. Nevertheless, although nothing definite was said about when and how the campaign for non-payment of taxes was to begin, the very slogan of non-payment was attractive enough for the peasantry.[12]

Gandhi is regarded categorically as a spent force in all articles written at this time, while gradually a growing hostility develops towards the constitutional Party of Das.

The Swaraj party, until now representing the most active part of the left-wing of the nationalist movement, now abandons its programme for independence and openly steps forward for self-government under the aegis of the British Empire. All resistance from the Indian bourgeoisie has ceased. All they want is the grant of a certain amount of participation in the exploitation of the Indian workers. On the other hand, it is becoming increasingly clear to the imperialists that they have need of the Indian bourgeoisie as an ally rather than at the head of the discontented elements which have to be watched and, at times, treated harshly. The epoch of differences between imperialism and native capitalism has come to an end. The

[12] *Kommunisticheski Internatsional* (1925), No. V, p. 152

> Swarajist . . . can be compared to the Cadet Party in Russia . . . henceforth, bourgeois nationalism will flow along the constitutional path of "the most loyal opposition of His Britannic Majesty".

The turning-point came in 1925. The second period of Soviet assessment of Gandhi began with a speech at the Communist University for the Toilers of the East in which Stalin stated:

> The basic and the new thing about the conditions existing in the colonies such as India is that not only has the national bourgeoisie split into the revolutionary wing and the wing which stood for agreement with the imperialists but that the treasonable part of the bourgeoisie has already come to such an agreement with Imperialism. Fearing revolution more than imperialism, fearing for the interest of their purse more than the interest of their own country, this, the richest and most influential part of the bourgeoisie, places both its feet firmly into the camp of the implacable enemies of the revolution, forming a block with the British against the workers and peasants of their own country. One cannot attain a victory for revolution without smashing this block.[13]

The pronouncement by the new master of Russia received specific application in 1928 in a resolution of the sixth meeting of the Comintern.

> The communists must unmask the reformism of the Indian National Congress and oppose all manifestations of Swarajism, Gandhism, etc., and all theories about passive resistance with the irreconcilable slogan of the struggle for the liberation of the country and expulsion of the imperialists.[14]

In 1930, at the XVIth Congress of the C.P.S.U., Stalin referred to Gandhi in person – "the bourgeois plan to fill these countries with bloodshed and to be protected by the bayonets of the police, depends upon the help of people like Gandhi".[15]

On the basis of this clear-cut directive, several monographs devoted specifically to Gandhi were written. It should be noted, however, that the entry on Gandhi in the Soviet Encyclopaedia, which went to press

[13] Stalin, *Sochineniya*, vol. 7, p. 147

[14] *VIth Meeting, Comintern*, Procès Verbal, p. 53

[15] Stalin, *op. cit.*, vol. 12, p. 252

on May 15th, 1929, shows that the new interpretation had not yet been fully assimilated. In this article the general view is still that of the first period. The Mahatma is seen as a spent force. His imprisonment in 1921 and the indifference to this by the masses, was interpreted as "the sad outcome of 10 years' struggle, which was not only his own personal tragedy but the unavoidable finale of the whole movement of liberation by the Indian bourgeoisie, torn apart by internal contradictions".[16] Statements occur in this article which were inconceivable at any later date before the death of Stalin; "until 1919", declares the author of the article with some boldness, "the Indian national movement, the kernel of which was Congress, was limited to the circles of the bourgeoisie and the intelligentsia. Gandhi accomplished the association with it of the million-fold mass of the peasants and workers." Neither Amritsar nor Bardoli are overstressed and a balanced account is given of Gandhi's activities in South Africa: "Repeated imprisonments, fines and beatings-up by white trash – nothing", the article declares, "could break the will of Gandhi." [17]

By the middle of the year, the position had changed completely – Stalin's thesis had been driven home. Henceforth, I have not come across any quotation or reference in Russian to Marx's "Letters on India" where the British are given the credit for breaking up the old feudal particularism and introducing railways and capital. "The political unity of India", wrote Marx, "was the first condition for its regeneration. That unity, imposed by the British sword, will be strengthened and perpetuated by the electric telegraph." [18] Since Stalin's pronouncement, however, the British influence was seen as entirely negative and harmful and likewise were all parties which objected to the use of violence against the imperialists. Gandhi was in this group.

A major article on Gandhism which appeared in *Revolyutsionny Vostok* of 1929 begins with a juxtaposition of quotations from Gandhi and Marx.

> Our forefathers knew that if we sought after machines, we would become slaves and would lose our spiritual character. Therefore, after serious consideration, they decided that we should make do with our own legs and arms, and they reasoned further that large

[16] *Bolshaya Sovyetskaya Entsiklopedia*, vol. XIV, p. 517

[17] *Ibid.*, p. 515

[18] Marx and Engels, *Selected Works* (Foreign Languages Publishing House), vol. I, p. 320

> towns were traps and a useless burden and that the people in them would not be happy – they would be full of thieves and plunderers, vice and prostitution would flourish there and the poor would be exploited by the wealthy.[19]

Then follows a quotation from Marx:

> These idyllic village communities, however harmless they might seem, were always the firm basis of oriental despotism. They delimited human reason within the narrowest confines, making of it a militant weapon of superstition, subordinating it to traditional rules, and depriving it of any historical significance.[20]

This sets the tone: Gandhism is a Right deviation.

Whereas before 1925 Gandhi was seen as categorically opposed to caste inequalities, the new view is that:

> Gandhi stands for the perpetuation of what is the basic source of inequality – the very institution of caste. For Gandhi knows that the prejudice of millions is a vast power. Gandhi is prepared to utilise the foulest remnant of the Indian middle ages – the caste prejudices of millions of Indians – so as to prevent somehow the penetration into holy India of the devilish civilisation of the modern world.[21]

Gandhi's closeness to Tolstoy is now turned against him.

> Religious morality, the primeval village, the spinning-wheel and home-woven cloth, just as its embodiment in passive resistance to evil – this is the symbol of the faith of Gandhism. Basically, these are the same traits which characterise Tolstoyism. One is, therefore, quite justified in applying to Gandhism the judgement given by Lenin on the teaching of Tolstoy. "The teaching of Tolstoy is undoubtedly utopian and, in its content, reactionary in the most exact meaning of the word." But in Tolstoy, the great artist, the critical element was at least strongly developed and this could, as Lenin showed, at a certain stage of development "in practice bring benefit to certain layers of the population, contrary to the reactionary and utopian traits of Tolstoyism".

[19] *Revolyutsionny Vostok* (1922), No. 7, *Gandhism*, p. 117
[20] *Ibid.* [21] *Ibid.*, p. 120

"Gandhi was no artist of the word, however," continues this article.

> His hatred of contemporary civilisation can be seen in his glorification of the past, instead of showing up the evils of capitalist society . . . In Gandhi one hardly finds a severe criticism of the imperialist exploitation of India, of the torment of the population by the police – in fact, of all that characterises a colonial regime. The critical elements in the teaching of Gandhi almost completely disappear. Therefore, it was precisely and only the reactionary aspect of Tolstoy's teaching that Gandhi took hold of and turned into a dogma.[22]

The author of the article goes into a lengthy historical explanation to account for the fact that "the teaching of Gandhi found its way into the midst of the Indian masses and became the ideology of millions".[23] The answer lies neither in coincidence nor in the personality or the teaching of Gandhi. It lies rather in the historical condition of India at the end of the first world war.

> In all classical capitalist countries, alongside the pauperisation of the peasantry and break-up of crafts, there existed the process of the rapid growth of urban industry which absorbed the mass of petty producers ejected from the country or craft and therefore becoming a proletariat.[24]

In India

> the whole process is more painful. Owing to the slow tempo of industrial development brought about by the policy of imperialism, the impoverished craftsman finds no place in an Indian factory and has to return to the over-populated village.

The bourgeoisie, which had originally been at one with the people in their opposition to the British, changed sides and came into league with the imperialists, when the decision had been taken by the government to abandon the policy of arresting Indian industrial development. The local craftsmen, severely hampered during the earlier stage by British imported manufactured goods, had not, in the pre-war period, been placed in a desperate position. The local crafts had not been killed. In 1911 there were still 17·5 million employed in handicrafts. Between

[22] *Revolyutsionny Vostok* (1922), No. 7, *Gandhism*, p. 117

[23] *Ibid.* [24] *Ibid.*, pp. 124, *et sec*

1911 and 1921, however, there was a catastrophic 12% drop in such employment as a result of severe competition from local industry. In the confusing economic situation which resulted, the people had no clear idea of their true enemy and it was this confusion which Gandhism was said to have reflected and thrived on.

There followed the "wild mixture of the most fanatical forms of conflict" – the Malabar Muslims fought the Hindus while the Akali sect fought for the reformation of the temples. "These same characteristics of confusion can be seen in the teaching of Gandhism." An elemental protest on the part of the small independent producer, expropriated and excluded from the productive process; the hate of the ruined craftsmen for the machine which is the direct cause of his misfortune; the confusion of the peasant, finding himself with his wife and children in a factory of the early capitalist epoch with its sixteen-hour day . . . the helplessness and the weakness of the atomised peasant mass before the blind force of capital – one of the most powerful in the world, armed to the teeth and prepared to use every means to maintain its sway.

> All this together [it was argued] is sufficient to explain the contradictions in the teaching of Gandhi, the idea of passive resistance, the rejection of modern society, of technical progress and class struggle and the idealisation of the ancient asiatic order. In all this, the ideology of Gandhism was a reflection of processes taking place in India at the time.

*But,*

> while reflecting in his teaching the ideology of the impoverished artisan and craftsman, Gandhi and his followers were, in their practical political activity, closely bound up with the native ruling class. Hence, the absence even of those critical elements which can be seen in Tolstoy. Hence also, Gandhism is a reactionary theory. Gandhism in action, the Gandhism which influenced the political action of the mass, was the greatest obstacle on the path of their liberation and became a counter-revolutionary force. To this, the history of the first Indian revolution is witness.

Gandhi, however, was worse than the Indian bourgeoisie – *his* betrayal of the working class dated from a period earlier still than the post-war crisis. It was already during his African period that

> Gandhi failed to put forward one single economic demand in the interest of the cruelly exploited coolies. On the contrary, all his efforts in Africa were directed towards restraining the workers from putting forward "unjust demands" so as to limit within the framework of a peaceful demonstration their growing hatred of the white settlers. The workers followed him in that there was no one who could dispel the lies and the reactionary teaching of Gandhi and could show to the workers the correct path.

Gandhi's Red Cross work is described as "actively helping English imperialism to devour the small independent republics". The early use of *satyagraha* among the coolies is discredited. It is shown to have coincided with a strike of white miners and railway workers. When it was proposed to Gandhi that the white workers should form a united front with the *satyagraphi*, not only did Gandhi refuse but, out of fear lest his strike be identified with that of the Europeans, he called off his own *satyagraha* campaign. "From that moment", the Russians cite Gandhi as saying, "Europeans and South Africans recognised *satyagraha* as a worthy and honourable movement – a constitutional movement." The Russians comment that

> to refuse help to the striking workers, to call off your own strikes only so that General Smuts – who was responsible for the anti-Indian legislation in South Africa – should recognise the movement as constitutional – one must confess, it is difficult to find anything more false, hateful or harmful to the interests of the working class than Gandhism.

The concept of civil disobedience strikes the Russians as completely ludicrous – they ridicule the very idea of a publisher's name and address appearing on so-called illegal documents.

> All this demonstration has as its aim merely to show to the world the purity of intention of the nationalists. In fact, this programme was intended only to frighten the government so as to obtain a change of atmosphere among the English rulers of India or, as Gandhi put it – so as to create the basis for an advantageous compromise with the imperialists.[25]

Hence, in the question of non-payment of taxes

> Gandhi fully understood that here he was playing with fire and

[25] *Revolyutsionny Vostok* (1922) No., 7, *Gandhism*, p. 133

subsequently treated the slogan in such a way as to reduce its revolutionary significance to nought. Including this slogan in his programme from the very beginning, it was only at the end of 1921 that Gandhi decided, after many waverings, to put it into action. However, even then, he took every measure to avoid revolutionary consequences. The peasantry was called to a refusal of tax payment only where it was wholly permeated by the idea of passive resistance.

In 1930 there appeared another large article entitled "Gandhi: Prophet of the Indian Bourgeoisie". Its main thesis is the same Stalinist view that Gandhism is just a kind of reformism to deflect the people's attention away from revolution.

> The practice and theory of Gandhism are that historically created weapon which the Indian bourgeois has fashioned for himself so as to guide the revolutionary movement on to a reformist path – in that only once they have been made harmless by the Gandhian teaching, dosed up with non-violence and non-resistance, distracted towards all kinds of symbolical actions and away from their direct class interests, can the masses be a support for the treacherous compromise of the bourgeoisie with imperialism.[26]

The author points at apparent contradictions in Gandhism which are to him absolute proof of its falsity. Gandhi, he said, claims to stand for non-violence and yet in the Boer War and the Great War he did not object to fighting. Gandhi pretends to object to modern industry and advocates the use of the spinning-wheel and yet he defends the high tariff which would protect nascent industries.

Gandhi adapts to the purpose of the bourgeoisie both the reactionary and the progressive tendencies of the peasantry.

> Accepting in full the reactionary aspect of the peasants' aspirations (spinning-wheel, hate of the town and industry), in the first place he puts the whole movement under the sign of non-violence; in the second place, in place of the reactionary demands of the peasants he substitutes petty-fogging reformist demands such as the lowering of the land tax and abolition of the salt-tax. Gandhi does not dare to attack caste divisions, he merely renovates them a little; Gandhi does not dare openly to attack the Indian oppressors and the foul exploitation of the people by the temples, but meekly asks the exploiters to

[26] *Kommunisticheski Internatsional* (1930), No. XV, p. 37

become just a tiny bit more progressive; Gandhi does not oppose superstitions and prejudices, but merely brings them up to date and paints them up in a bourgeois manner. In place of the "new sky and a new earth" propounded by the French bourgeoisie in its revolutionary years the prophet of the Indian bourgeoisie has to be born a saint and a man of fasts, has to stand out in defence of exploitation and caste, shamefacedly has to idealise the revolting asiatic quality of the Indian middle ages – in all this is the unavoidable pomade, the trappings of the deception, fooling, and disorientation of the Indian peasant and artisan.[27]

The author quotes Gandhi as saying that "I know that the government fears only the people over whom I have an apparent influence. The Anglo-Indian government does not suspect that I fear the masses as much as it does itself." [28]

The *satyagraha* campaign of 1930 was interpreted within the broader context of the world economic crisis and the Indian industrialists' demand for a lowering of the rupee exchange rate as well as the erection of a protective tariff barrier.

The crisis which painfully hit the dividends of Indian industrialists, already aggravated by the British financial policy, the stormy growth of petty bourgeois discontent, the distinct increase in peasant unrest and finally the apprehension that if it were not headed by the treacherous leadership of national reformism, then it would be led by other forces – such were the motives of the new left manœuvre of Gandhi and Congress. Gandhi spent a whole month thinking out what character to give to the campaign of civil resistance so as to avoid the horrors of Chauri Chaura – the horrors of a wide revolutionary development of the peasant movement. Finally, after careful consideration, the salt monopoly was selected as the object of the campaign of non-compliance. This had the advantage over the land tax campaign of 1922, that the possibility was avoided of a refusal by the peasantry to pay not only tax but rent to the landlord.[29]

Once this viewpoint had been accepted, it was not long before the Communist Party of India was formed. In these circumstances, the advocates of what Kautsky in his recent book[30] conveniently labels

[27] *Kommunisticheski Internatsional* (1930). No. XV, p. 37
[28] *Ibid.* [29] *Ibid.*
[30] J. H. Kautsky, *Moscow and the Communist Party of India* (New York, 1956)

the "Right-policy" – and consequently a pro-Gandhi policy – were purged. Roy, author of *India in Transition*, who was much read in Russia, found himself in this group.

> Roy's conception, his valuation of class forces and the tactic he proposes are petty-menshevik. This is most clearly seen in that he accords to the proletariat in action solely the role of the left flank of a national-bourgeois front directed and headed by the treasonable bourgeoisie. The group of Roy places before the proletariat the task merely of criticising the mistakes of the bourgeoisie and exerting a certain amount of pressure through its left wing.[31]

By the mid-thirties, apprehensions begin to creep into Soviet articles on India lest the old Gandhism, which was for so long described as effete, should be regenerated by the Congress Socialist Party.

> In the course of many years bourgeois nationalism exploited the oppressed and low state of the people, the patriarchal-peasant belief in the utility of "rebelling by standing on one's knees", the subconscious faith of the masses in the upper strata of the bourgeoisie in order to weaken and to divert the mass anti-imperialist struggle, at every step betraying the people. The teaching of non-violence was a means to this end.[32]

Now, however, the position is seen to have altered.

> The upshot of the economic crisis was believed to be that the people had become politically more articulate and were turning more decisively to the left. Therefore, congressional pseudo-socialism was sent to help out traditional Gandhism. All that happened was that Gandhism expanded the extent of its promises. Not only independence but socialism, ready-made and tidy, complete with "authority for the producing masses" with socialisation of industry and banks and even with collectivisation of agriculture . . . all obtainable by means of the same universal measure of non-violence.
>
> An anti-imperialist revolution together with an anti-feudal revolution and even a socialist upheaval – all flow together into one heavenly mistiness. Why should the workers quarrel with the capitalists? Why should the peasants raise their hands against the landowners? Why embark on the struggle against imperialism when all

[31] Programa i Praktika Renegatskoi Grupy Roya in *Revolyutsionny Vostok*, XIII–XVI (1932), p. 206

[32] *Kommunisticheski Internatsional* (1934), No. 30

this can be prevented in a legal and peaceful way? One need only add a plea for socialism to the plea for independence. The whole dance of this newly arrived congressional socialism is linked with traditional Gandhism. Its tightrope stretches from *purna swaraj* and non-violence to *swadeshi*, to the demand for the use of only locally produced national goods. On this tightrope there balance the acrobats of congress-socialism armed with all these popular sounding ideas about collectivisation and a planned economy. Let us stick a socialist label on *swadeshi*, they say, it will help Indian capital in its struggle for the internal market against Lancashire and Japanese production. The workers can be told that the capitalists will become kinder if the whole nation becomes one large trading concern.[33]

In spite of this hostility towards him, Gandhi's arrest in 1932 was seen by *Pravda* as "a new offensive by British imperialism against the toilers of India".[34] This extraordinary piece of double-think is supported by the Machiavellian theory that the British authorities arrested Gandhi and the other Congress leaders in order to raise their prestige in the eyes of the masses and thus prevent the people from following more revolutionary leaders.

Between 1935 and the death of Stalin the attitude to Gandhi, so far as I have been able to see, remained basically the same and unchanged in spite of the fact that the policy towards bourgeois parties in the colonies went through several clear-cut phases, as has been shown by Kautsky in his excellent book, *Moscow and the Communist Party of India*.

Kautsky labels the two distinct strategies as the "left" and the "right". The "left" strategy envisaged a socialist revolution as its immediate goal, while the "right" strategy regarded as its main enemy not capitalism but foreign imperialism. The first envisaged a social revolution; the latter a national one. From the seventh Congress of the Comintern in 1935 until 1947 a "right" strategy was followed. There was some wavering. Before the German invasion of Russia, for instance, Congress was supported in its resistance to involvement in the war. Conspicuous in this respect was an article in *Pravda* on 16th November 1939. On the other hand, once the war had become patriotic rather than imperialist –

[33] *Kommunisticheski Internatsional* (1934), No. 30
[34] See *Manchester Guardian*, 6 January 1932

after the Nazi attack on USSR – it is reported, but I have not seen this reference myself, that Gandhi was criticised for being anti-British and sabotaging the "people's war". The few references I have seen to Gandhi during this period invariably follow the pattern I have outlined.

In 1947, at the Congress of the Soviet Academy of Sciences, there took place a disagreement between the adherents of "left" and "right" strategies. One view, represented by academicians Dyakov and Balabushevich, identified the entire bourgeoisie in colonial countries with imperialism and favoured the return to a left strategy. Opposed to this view was that of Zhukov, director of the Academy's Pacific Institute who condemned only the "big" bourgeoisie.

In this controversy, however, Gandhi was attacked by both wings – he was just as much anathema to the right group as to the left. Zhukov wrote in an article outlining his views in *Mirovoye Khoziaistvo i Mirovaya Politika*, July 1947:

> The activity of the Indian working class, its active role in the struggle against English hegemony, pushed the "big" bourgeoisie all the more firmly into the camp of reaction and impelled it to take up anti-national positions. Hence, the support by Indian industrial magnates of the ideology of Gandhism which poisons the masses with disbelief in their own strength, which propagates non-resistance to evil by violence, disarming the masses morally and ideologically. Gandhism is an ideal system for covering up a deal between the imperialists and the feudalists. It is quite natural that the "big" bourgeoisie grasps at the teaching of Gandhi because it fully justifies its position, its desire to find a means of agreeing with British imperialism. Apostle of Indian backwardness, opponent of industrialization, bard of the spinning-wheel and the miserable wattle-hut, Gandhi's standpoint of non-resistance to evil by force leads one to certain considerations. One should make acquaintance with the evidence of the historian of Congress, Pattabhi Sitaramayya who wrote a book about Gandhi and carefully examined his whole life. This historian of Congress tells the following: "When certain right wing congress circles began calling for the creation of 'self-defence' units against the communists and began to recommend that the members of these units should have training in the use of arms, certain orthodox Gandhians doubted the correctness of these measures. They went to Gandhi for advice and the Mahatma replied,

'Yes certainly, non-resistance is better than violence, but violence is better than cowardice . . .' This means that when imperialism is discussed, non-resistance is recommended, but when the question concerns the fight against communism, violence is permissible. To this day, Gandhi plays a negative, arresting role in the development of India and Indian social thought. The demonstrative democratism of Gandhi is seen in that he travels third-class, mixing in this way with the simple people. But Gandhi is deeply hostile to the people in that he is against progressive changes made by the people. His verbal attack on the caste system in fact covers up his support for it." [35]

No opportunity for propaganda was missed – even if it was inconsistent with the general line held at a particular time. For instance, in spite of the official doctrine that Gandhi was a British stooge, the *Literaturnaya Gazeta* commented on his assassination that the suggestion that the British Secret Service was connected with the shooting, was not without foundation:

> The British and American press raised the cry that the murder of Gandhi was the meaningless crime of a fanatic. No. The killing of Gandhi has meaning . . . of late Gandhi was using his authority to prevent the internecine war which was artificially fomented in India by the British and by Attlee and Bevin, those trusty agents of British imperialism. The death of Gandhi was necessary to the British imperialists as proof that they were right. They calculated to use the death of Gandhi for further inflaming internecine strife.[36]

This was repeated by Moscow Radio. However, Louis Fischer reports[37] that the Soviet delegate at the Security Council spoke favourably of the dead leader when presumably it was impolitic for him to dissent on this matter from his colleagues on the Council.

In 1948 Dyakov, belonging to the opposite, left wing camp, published his work on *The National Question and British Imperialism in India*. Looking back over the period of "right" strategy during the war which, in the light of Zhdanov's speech at the opening of the Cominform, he now thought was about to come to an end, Dyakov wrote that

[35] *Mirovoye Khoziastvo i Mirovaya Politika* (July 1947), p. 7
[36] See *New York Times*, 5 February 1948
[37] Louis Fischer, *Life of Gandhi*, p. 23

The National Congress enjoyed great influence in the country. *But* even in those periods when the communists had actively participated in the organisation and when it was a block of anti-imperialist parties its leadership remained bourgeois. The Gandhian tactic of the envolvement of the masses in the struggle, its call for a refusal to use violence against the English oppressors, gave to the bourgeoisie the possibility of utilising the movement of the masses to exert pressure on the English ruling class without endangering their position in the country. Advocating non-violence in the struggle of the masses for liberation, Gandhi did not come forward against the oppression of the masses by the imperialists but rather justified the forcible suppression of the mass movement by the police, when the labouring people actively came forward against the imperialists. *If* the Gandhian teaching had originally had a certain progressive significance, facilitating an awakening of the masses from complete political apathy and passivity, then, at a later stage, Gandhism became the basic ideological weapon of the bourgeoisie for the subjection of the masses to their influence and a prime brake on the awakening of the class consciousness of the workers. The left-wing phraseology of Nehru created an aura of revolution around the bourgeois leadership of Congress and helped in the establishment among the masses of an illusion as to the community of interests of all Indian classes against British oppression.[38]

By the middle of 1949 Moscow decided that a "left" strategy would divert parties away from the struggle against the Anglo-American *bloc*. On June 7, 8 and 9 *Pravda* published Liu Shao Chi's assertion that Asian communist parties could cooperate with the bourgeoisie. In spite of Ranadive's growing intransigence, it seemed that Moscow had made the decision to play down the class struggle in India and to use this newly independent neighbour in its front against the Western powers. On January 27, 1950, the Cominform journal told the CPI to take the Chinese path and to make a broad united front with the anti-imperialist classes. After a repetition of the same advice by Dutt in December 1950, Ranadive was replaced by Rao and in April 1951 the CPI rejected guerrilla warfare as a means of policy.

Nevertheless, however, this *detente* – far from heralding a more realistic assessment of the recently assassinated Gandhi – coincided with

[38] A. Dyakov, *Natsionalny Vopros i Angliisky Imperialism v Indii*, 1948, p. 33

a very definite intensification of the struggle against him. Three monographs about the Mahatma appeared during 1952: Reisner's *New History of the Countries of the Non-Soviet East*, the revised entry in Volume 10 of the *Large Soviet Encyclopaedia* and a new book by Dyakov on *India During and After the Second World War*. This latter book is of particular interest in that it bears all the marks of being a hasty expression of a re-emphasised policy from above. My impression is that it was originally written in conformity with the Zhukovite line (the so-called 'neo-Maoist') of 1949 but that a hostile statement on Gandhi and Congress had been made meanwhile probably by Stalin himself at a late stage in the preparation of the book. The volume has an introduction in which the author – referring to himself in the third person – confesses his errors:

> The author [Dyakov writes of himself] over-estimated the depth of the contradictions between the monopolist top of the Indian bourgeoisie and English imperialism and underestimated the connection of this top with the British imperialists and with their basic support – the feudal princes and landowners whose role in Congress was thereby decreased. The author distinguished insufficiently clearly the contradictions between the top and the major part of the national bourgeoisie and in a number of his works saw the bourgeoisie of colonial India as an undifferentiated whole.
>
> Speaking of growing contradictions between the major Indian bourgeoisie and English imperialism, the author relegated to a secondary plane the other more important tendency, the increased striving of the monopolist top of the Indian bourgeoisie towards agreement with the English imperialists along with the strengthening of class contradictions and the development of the national liberation struggle in accordance with a sharpening of class struggles.
>
> The author has incorrectly assessed Congress as a block of anti-imperialist parties. This assessment was clearly mistaken.[39]

Finally, he marks the nadir of Gandhi's reputation in Russia when he states:

> Apart from these basic mistakes, there are other shortcomings and incorrect formulations in the words of the author. Thus, alongside the correct view of the reactionary nature of Gandhism, he wrote

[39] A. Dyakov, *India vo Vremya i Posle Vtoroi Mirovoi Voiny* (1952), p. ii

incorrectly that Gandhism, even in its earliest stages, played a progressive role in helping the political awakening of the masses.

In the body of the book, needless to say, no positive role whatsoever has been allowed to remain to Gandhi. He cannot be compared to Sun Yat Sen who did have a positive role.

> This cannot be said of Gandhi and Gandhism. If Gandhi helped to turn Congress into a mass organisation and to attract the popular masses to participation in *satyagraha*, *hartals* and the boycotts and brought them close to political struggle, then, at the same time, politically, he subjected these masses to the major bourgeoisie, brought them up in a spirit of slavish reformism, impeded the development of the class struggle and thereby the conversion of the Indian mass liberation movement into an anti-imperialist revolution. Gandhi never was a revolutionary. He was always an active and irreconcilable enemy of revolution.[40]

The arguments concerning the one-sided application of Gandhi's theories about violence recur:

> always and everywhere Gandhi found justification for the exploiters and oppressors when they carried out the worst violence on the people and, at the same time, opposed the least protest of the down-trodden who are actively coming forward against their oppressors. Not once did Gandhi appear with an equally merciless condemnation of the violence committed at every step in India by the British as he came out against the few examples of violence committed by the Indians who, when brought to extremes, tried to defend their lives and rights by force . . . this one-sided condemnation is the most characteristic trait of Gandhi . . . during the lifetime of Gandhi the large Indian bourgeoisie and the liberal landowners still needed the support of the mass movement and therefore they utilised the passive and peaceful struggle of the people to exert pressure on English imperialism. But after the final agreement with the British and the change over to the camp of reaction, the large bourgeoisie began more than ever before to push forward the first aspect of Gandhi's teaching – his condemnation of any violence by the masses against their oppressors, his justification of any kind of action so long as it was carried out on the basis of law, custom and traditions even if

[40] A. Dyakov, *op cit.*, p. 162

these customs were forced on India by her oppressors. It gave the leadership of Congress a weapon with which to split the worker movement and the peasant unions.[41]

The familiar argument goes on for pages but what is new here is the piece of mumbo-jumbo which is dragged in to justify all this:

> The Gandhian teaching grew up as an ideological superstructure on the basis representing the union of an ugly colonial capitalism in the cities with feudal relics reigning in the country. In that this basis has remained in India till the present time, the teaching of Gandhi is being used by the exploiting classes for a strengthening and support of the old basis. In his work of genius concerning "Marxism in Linguistics" Stalin wrote "the superstructure is borne by the basis but this does not at all mean that it only reflects the basis, that it is passive, neutral, regards the fate of its own basis with indifference. On the contrary, appearing in the world it becomes the greatest motive power actively helping its basis to assert itself and strengthen its position, taking every measure to help the new order to liquidate and finish off the old basis and the old classes.[42]

Even Gandhi's efforts to quell the Muslim-Hindu riots are given an ulterior motive:

> the position adopted by Gandhi is explicable by the fact that the pogroms took threatening proportions and came to aggravate the already considerable economic disorder of the country.[43]

These naïve and unsubtle arguments are repeated by Reisner, but with a liberal admixture of puerile abuse. For instance, " 'The salvation of India,' *croaked Gandhi*, 'lies in forgetting all that she has learnt in the past fifty years . . .' Gandhi was said to have 'aped the ascetics'." [44]

A similar caricature of Gandhi appeared in the large Soviet Encyclopaedia. By 1954 translations of it reached India, unfortunately precisely at the time of Nehru's visit to Peking and the opening of the new Soviet leaders' campaign to win the confidence of the under-developed countries. Letters poured into the Indian press.

> The above citations wrote [an outraged correspondent to *The Hindu*] prove that either the Soviet writers are misinformed about Gandhi and India or else they are deliberately distorting facts to suit

[41] A. Dyakov, *op. cit.*, p. 162 [42] *Ibid.* [43] *Ibid.*

[44] I. Reisner, *Novaya Istoria Zarubezhnovo Vostoka* (1952), p. 299

> their pet theories . . . will the communists of India give their reaction to the observations of the Soviet encyclopaedia on Gandhi? Here is a test of their emotional attachment to India and her great leader to which Mr Nehru recently referred.[45]

A leading article in *The Hindu* deplored the "fantastically tendencious and perverted account of Gandhi current in the Soviet Union. This was proof", the paper held, that "respect for objective truth is not one of the communist virtues and the distortion of facts to suit the Stalinist thesis has been practised in various forms for over three decades."

To say the very least, the continuance of this Stalinist interpretation of Gandhi would have been most damaging to the Russian cause at a time when India was being courted with offers of steel-mills and technical assistance. It was impossible for the Russian government to continue wooing India on the one hand (giving Indians Stalin Peace Prizes and fussing over troupes of Indian dancers) and, on the other hand, to go on piling insult on the past injuries inflicted on Gandhi. The *Manchester Guardian* described the publication of the article in the encyclopaedia as "a grave blunder. Such small but telling episodes in Indo-Soviet relations have far more lasting and damaging effects than the reports never quite believed, of forced labour camps and brain-washing behind the Iron Curtain." [46]

Something had to change. The Indian Government protested to the Soviet Embassy that such a false account was "completely opposed to the professed Soviet friendship and respect for India".[47]

In December, Kozhevnikov, the Soviet constitutional historian on a goodwill delegation to India, promised to see that this incorrect entry was corrected.

> Lenin [he said] did not agree with the philosophy of Tolstoy, and yet he wrote many articles acknowledging Tolstoy's genius and greatness. Even if the authors of the encyclopaedia did not agree with certain aspects of Gandhi's philosophy, they had no right to make uncomplimentary remarks about him.

Now the final – and one might almost say revolutionary reassessment of Gandhi took place at the end of 1955. It is amusing, in parenthesis, to recall that only a few months after the appearance of the

[45] *The Hindu*, 13 October 1954

[46] *The Manchester Guardian*, 20 October 1954

[47] *The Observer*, 31 October 1954

encyclopaedia, Krishna Menon, the Indian Ambassador, had presented to the Soviet Academy of Sciences a valuable edition of the works of Gandhi. This was ceremonially accepted with thanks. However, the first real hint of the new view was an article in *Kommunist.* The Mahatma is described (curiously enough together with Ataturk) as a "progressive" leader, though in his lifetime he was only the "spiritual leader of India". This was an indication of the shape of things to come. In his speech before the Indian parliament on November 21, Bulganin said:

> The Soviet people sincerely sympathise with the devoted and courageous struggle waged by your people against colonial oppression. We know how greatly important in that struggle were the ideas and guidance of the distinguished leader of the Indian national movement, Mahatma Gandhi. (Prolonged applause).[48]

At the XXth Congress of the Communist Party of the USSR, Kuusinnen went a stage further, asking for a reassessment. He said that

> Messrs Khruschev and Bulganin had quite rightly recognised in their speeches in India the prominent role played by Mahatma Gandhi in the history of the Indian people. Thereby Messrs Bulganin and Khruschev took upon themselves the task of correcting those mistakes which in previous years had found expression in the works of Soviet orientalists and in *Kommunisticheski Internatsional.* Basing themselves exclusively on criticism of the philosophical views of Gandhi – which, as is well-known, are widely different from those of Marxism and Leninism – some of our publicists went to such an extreme of one-sidedness that they absolutely denied Gandhi any positive historical role.
>
> I want to add here [he continued] that our historians and propagandists have reason critically to examine certain other of our views – for instance, the well-known theses of the VIth Congress of the Comintern on colonial questions. Concretely, I have in mind in these theses, the characterisation and assessment of the role of the national bourgeoisie in colonial and semi-colonial countries.[49]

Six weeks after this speech, *Sovyetskoye Vostokovedeniye* published a

[48] *Visit of Friendship* (Foreign Languages Publishing House 1956), p. 25

[49] *Stenograficheski Otchet XX ovo Kongressa KPSS*, vol. I, p. 503

leading article on "The XXth Congress of the C.P.S.U. and Problems of the Study of the East". Here it was stated

> of course, Soviet orientalists do not share the philosophical outlook of Gandhism. On the other hand, this in no way, precludes an acknowledgement of the major and positive role of Gandhi in the history of the struggle of the Indian people.[50]

In November 1956, a long article appeared in *Sovyetskoye Vostokovedeniye* entitled "The Role of Gandhi in the National Liberation Movement of the Peoples of India". This went further still, amounting to a complete rehabilitation of Gandhi. Curiously enough, the article is by Dyakov and Reisner – until recently the most vehement enemies of Gandhi. Interesting also is that this was the second time that Dyakov was publicly making a *volte-face* and confessing his error. The article falls into two parts – firstly a round-up on the Soviet view of India in general, and secondly a study on Gandhi.

It is argued that two fundamental errors underline the Stalinist view on India. In the first place, the successes attained by the National Liberation movement under the leadership of Congress were very small.

> The objective facts about the development of India show that the working class did not become the controlling factor in the national liberation movement and that the leading role belonged to the bourgeoisie. Soviet indologists considered that the liberation of India could take place only under the leadership of the proletariat. Since the proletariat had to struggle for hegemony against the bourgeoisie, the bourgeoisie – and consequently Congress and Gandhi – were looked upon as forces obstructing the development of the liberation movement. Such dogmatic mistakes were admitted by the authors of the present article . . . there were correct assessments of the struggle against imperialism but even in this case, we could not avoid a certain one-sidedness. The national liberation struggle which culminated in independence, took place under the leadership of Congress. We overestimated the role of the working class and the C.P. and depicted the desirable as the actual. . . . In fact, it was the national bourgeoisie and its political leaders who, in spite of their fear of violent forms of revolutionary struggle, lead the masses in this conflict. . . . Of course, such armed risings as that of the sailors in

[50] *Sovyetskoye Vostokovedeniye*, No. I (1956), p. 8

> Bombay or the peasants in Telengana, the Tebhaga movement in Bengal, did play an important part in the liberation of India. But, local risings would not have shaken British rule if they had not taken place against the background of the non-violent mass movement of the workers, peasants and intelligentsia which seized hold of the whole community.[51]

In the second place, Soviet historians are held to have been wrong in thinking that the attainment of independence in 1947 was the result of a deal between the British and the bourgeois parties whereby India became a semi-colony of the U.K. "Temporary agreements between the imperialists and the national bourgeoisie did take place but the main line of development went in the direction of an intensification and a sharpening of class conflicts." Unlike China, where political control was divided between the imperialists and the national bourgeoisie, in India colonial pressure weighed not only on the labourers but on the whole bourgeoisie, including its upper layers. Therefore the national bourgeoisie had the possibility of speaking for the whole people. Under these conditions, the division of anti-imperialist forces along class lines was held up.

At this stage it is perhaps better to summarise the main points made in the reassessment of Gandhi himself.

1. The Soviet view of *Satyagraha*, which had previously often been regarded as passivity and non-resistance, was now corrected.

> Gandhi [wrote the authors] advocated not non-resistance but rather non-violent resistance – he never called upon the masses to stand aside from the struggle but he sought by every means to give to his mass movement a peaceful, non-violent character which corresponded with the interest of the Indian bourgeoisie which feared a sharpening of class conflicts.

2. In certain Soviet works Gandhi had been seen as the ally and often the agent of British imperialism. Such an assessment was made by Stalin at the XVIth Congress of the C.P.S.U.

> This judgement [states the article] was never correct. Gandhi was undoubtedly a patriot devoted to the task of liberating his country. Those of his actions with which we cannot agree are characterised by his views as representative of his class, the class of the national

[51] *Sovyetskoye Vostokovedeniye*, No. 5 (1956), p. 23

> bourgeoisie. These, however, cannot be seen as treasonable actions committed in the interests of imperialism.

3. A return is made to the pre-1925 view in seeing as Ghandi's main accomplishment the fact that he drew the masses into the independence movement.

4. Gandhi fought for the independent economic and political development of India. He did not put forward straight away the slogan of complete independence and often expressed indifference to the question whether India would reach full independence or acquire dominion status. But he was certain "that even if she receives only dominion status, India would eventually obtain independence".

5. For the first time, personal factors are touched upon:

> Unlike the moderate leaders of national congress who were violent partisans of European education and looked with contempt upon Indian culture and likewise upon traditional ideas and prejudices, Gandhi in his way of life, in his food and clothes, held to an ascetic simplicity. He refused a meat diet, and ate the same as the Indian peasants.

No more of his "aping the ascetics".

6. Now the authors fall over backwards to regard as a positive factor what had earlier been the very worst aspect of Gandhism. This was Gandhi's objection to Western technology.

> Preserving many patriarchal illusions, the peasantry – and particularly its more backward elements – saw the separate results of capitalist development as deeply alien phenomena forcibly thrust on India. Resistance to colonialism was equated in their consciousness with the struggle against capitalism. Many of these peasant ideas were taken up by Gandhi and we do not doubt his sincere conviction in the superiority of the hand spinning-wheel over the steam Jenny, primitive potions over modern medicine, the wooden over the tractor-driven plough. *But* it was precisely the anti-capitalist and religious façade of the ideology of Indian bourgeois nationalism which it received in the teaching of Gandhi which made it intelligible and acceptable to the multi-million masses of the patriarchal peasantry of India.

7. Another progressive aspect was Gandhi's resistance to the British

policy of playing off Muslims against Hindus. The rapprochement of Congress and the Muslim League and the taking-over of the Caliphate movement are seen as master-strokes of Gandhi. The blame for the failure of the wartime negotiations with Jinnah for uniting to press for an Indian government responsible to the legislative assembly cannot, according to this article, in any way be placed on Gandhi.

8. At long last there is a less perverted version of Gandhi's views on the caste system:

> He quite rightly considered the caste system to be one of the worst remnants of the past which impeded the unification of the Indian people in their struggle for liberation. He came forward against the attempt of the British to separate the untouchables from the general movement by placing them into a separate electoral curia. Owing to his influence among the Hindus and particularly among the untouchables, he was able to secure the rejection of this decision. He likewise waged a struggle for a repeal of the law forbidding untouchables to visit Hindu temples. Gandhi's campaign against untouchability had a great significance in subverting the bases of this institution and the caste system in general. It was not easy for Gandhi to secure support for this campaign within Congress. A large part of the party – and particularly its leaders – belonged to high castes. A contemptuous view of the untouchables permeated their very blood and bone. However, by ceaseless propaganda Gandhi accomplished a great deal in the weakening of caste.

9. Gandhi played a positive role in developing the movement for the self-determination of different peoples in India . . . at a time when there were quite a few people in Congress who did not favour the creation of national linguistic provinces, Gandhi came forward for a realisation of their demands. It is pointed out that

> the demand for the formation of national provinces had a progressive, democratic character in that it was directed against that system of administrative division of India created by British imperialism which impeded the political, economic and cultural development of its peoples.

10. In spite of the limited nature of his own economic programme, the authors consider that, "his negative attitude to the industrialisation of India did not, in spite of all Gandhi's influence, have a decisive

effect upon the economic programme of Congress", for Nehru understood that India could never be independent without an industry of its own.

In their summing-up the authors of this article give probably the best statement of the present Soviet view.

> Basically, Gandhi's was a positive role in the development of the national liberation movement. It was as a result of the activity of Gandhi as leader of Congress that this organization became a mass party. Our decidedly negative attitude to the non-violent tactic of Gandhi has been disproved by events.
>
> Of course, Gandhi was unwaveringly loyal to the tactic of non-violent resistance and this was often exploited by the imperialists in their own interest. This was the case in periods of temporary compromises which Gandhi reached with the government . . . however, Gandhi – and Congress under his leadership – succeeded in their main objective. Even though it was divided, India attained independence and became one of the important arbiters of peace in the world and in the struggle against colonialism.

The Soviet historians have come full circle.[52]

[52] At a meeting of Soviet Oriental specialists held in Tashkent in 1956 the question underwent further discussion. "Some oriental experts dogmatically applied the theses of Marxist-Leninist teaching to the live practice of the national liberation movement of the peoples of the East. Mention was made in a number of historical works about the hegemony of the proletariat in the national liberation struggle in countries where, in fact, no such proletariat existed. . . . They did not see that at a certain historical stage the national bourgeoisie can play a progressive role." *Sovremenny Vostok* (1957), No. 2, p. 45

# THE RISE AND SECESSION OF THE CONGRESS SOCIALIST PARTY OF INDIA (1934–1948)

*By Hari Kishore Singh*

THE FAILURE OF the 1930 and 1932 Civil Disobedience Movements, together with the breakdown of the two Round Table Conferences, created an atmosphere of dejection and despondency in India. Mahatma Gandhi had proclaimed his intention to devote himself to what he called 'constructive works', and this strengthened the belief that the national movement had a bleak future. Many interpreted the withdrawal of the Mahatma from active politics as proof of the failure of non-violent methods to achieve national independence. In this atmosphere of disappointment and disillusion two embryonic trends were noticeable.

First, there appeared an influential group of Congress leaders who as 'constitutionalists' were prepared to participate in the Assembly elections provided for by the Joint Parliamentary Committee's recommendations. For this purpose, they endeavoured to revive the old Swaraj Party.

Secondly, there developed amongst the general mass of younger Congressmen, who were by no means in agreement on ideological issues, a strong feeling that the Congress answer to the new situation should be the adoption of a really militant policy. Within this group were men who had either come under Marxist influence or who had imbibed social democratic ideas from Western countries. Broadly speaking, all of them could be called socialist in outlook. They had always been sceptical about Gandhi's ideas and his particular technique of national struggle, but owing to the prestige of the Mahatma they had reluctantly felt that the Civil Disobedience Movements should be given a fair trial. By 1934 these left-wing elements within Congress had become thoroughly persuaded that Gandhian methods of struggle were likely to be totally ineffective.

Now at this time support for the peasants and workers in their economic and social demands was bound to antagonise landlord and vested interests within Congress, since it would necessarily raise the issue of class struggle. The prospect of such a conflict was most unwelcome to many Congress leaders as was well appreciated by Jawaharlal Nehru, himself a socialist:

> The Congress as a whole, was a purely nationalist body, and included many middling Zamindars, and a few of the larger ones also. Its leaders were terribly afraid of anything which might raise the class issue, or irritate the Zamindar elements. So, right through the first six months of civil disobedience, they avoided calling for a general no-tax campaign in the rural areas, although conditions for this seemed to me to be ripe. I was not afraid of raising the class issue in this or any other way, but I recognised that the Congress, being what it was, could not then patronise class conflict.[1]

The right-wing elements in the Congress therefore tended to pin their faith for the immediate future in a revival of the Swaraj Party. But this was regarded as a retrogressive step by the left wing, who were convinced that since the deaths of C. R. Das and Motilal Nehru, who had led the party in the Bengal and Central legislatures, the party had lost its glamour and had quite ceased to put up a militant opposition. Though it might well continue to appeal to moderates, it had little to offer for the future.[2]

The left wing regarded the economic policy of the old Swaraj Party as essentially unprogressive, and judging from one of its election manifestos, they were probably right:

> We must supplement the work of the Congress by helping the labour and peasant organisations throughout the country. The problem of labour is always a difficult problem to some in every country, but in India the difficulties are greater. On the one hand,

[1] Jawaharlal Nehru, *An Autobiography*, p. 232

[2] At the Foundation Conference of the C.S.P. at Patna, 1934, Acharya Narendra Deva expressed the Left wing reaction to the proposed revival of the Swaraj Party when he declared: "I have a genuine fear that being deprived of the healthy influence of the revolutionary movement, the autonomous Swarajist organisation will, in course of time, become a *pucca* (full proof) constitutional and reformist body and will run counter to the revolutionary policy of the Congress." Acharya Narendra Deva, *Socialism and National Revolution*, p. 26

we must find out organisations by which we can prevent exploitation of labour by capitalists or landlords, but on the other hand, we must be on our guard to see that these organisations may not themselves be the source of oppression by nourishing extravagant and unreasonable demands.

Labour undoubtedly requires protection, but so also do industrial enterprises. Our organisation must protect both from exploitation, and the Trade Union Congress must be so organised as to be able to serve this useful purpose. We hold that in the long run the real interests of both and of the country at large are identical.[3]

Such doctrines of class harmony, similar to those preached by Gandhi, were unlikely to appeal to young socialists who, under Marxist influences, had convinced themselves of the inevitability of the class struggle. What is more, there were Swarajists themselves who were not convinced by the doctrine of class harmony. At a conference of the "Constitutionalists" held in May 1934, M. R. Masani urged members to undertake the organisation of peasants and workers in order to strengthen the struggle against British imperialism. The opposition to this proposal confirmed the existing suspicions of the left wing of the 'reactionary character' of the proposed party and of the undesirability of its revival. Indeed, the agreement reached at the All-Party Conference in 1928 on the question of property rights had already been a clear indication of the attitude of the right-wing leaders of the Congress to economic problems. On that occasion they had declared that 'all titles to private and personal property lawfully acquired at the establishment of the Commonwealth (i.e. independence) are hereby guaranteed'.

The leading figures in the revived Swaraj Party, Dr Ansari, K. M. Munshi, Bhulabhai Desai and B. C. Roy, were all well known for their orthodox conservative ideas on social and economic problems, and thus the attempted rejuvenation of the party gave little comfort to radical and socialist elements in the national movement.

Nevertheless, the Swaraj Party leaders were successful in winning the approbation of Mahatma Gandhi. In a statement after a meeting with the Mahatma, Dr Ansari declared:

He considers it right and the duty of Congressmen who were not offering Civil resistance and who believed in work in legislatures to

[3] Pattabhi Sitaramayya, *History of the Indian National Congress*, vol. I, p. 274

> prosecute the programme which they believe to be in the interests of the country. He goes even further and promises at all times to render such assistance to the Swaraj Party as lies in his power to give.[4]

Gandhi's favourable response to the overtures of the Swaraj Party was a further disillusionment to the militant left-wing Congressmen. They were already intensely angry with him for the quaint reasons he had given for the suspension of the Civil Disobedience Movement in 1933.[5] Jawaharlal Nehru had described these as 'an insult to the intelligence' and 'an amazing performance' for the leader of a national movement. Another leader, Subhas Bose, in a joint statement with the essentially moderate Vitthalbhai Patel, saw in the suspension of the Civil Disobedience Movement an outright 'confession of failure'. These two leaders made the following significant declaration:

> We are clearly of the opinion that Mr Gandhi as a political leader has failed. The time has come for a radical reorganisation of the Congress on a new method, for which a new leader is essential.

A source of fundamental disagreement between the socialists and Gandhi was his conception of 'trusteeship', according to which landlords and capitalists were merely trustees of the wealth of society and were to use it judiciously and wisely for the general well-being of the whole community.[6]

This implicit defence of the Zamindari system was a matter of great concern to the left wingers and they lost no opportunity of condemning it. Nehru's reaction against 'trusteeship' was representative of the whole left-wing approach when he confessed that:

> What upset me much more was Gandhiji's defence of the Zamindari

[4] See also Mahatma Gandhi's letter to Dr Ansari, *Modern Review*, May 1934

[5] When suspending the Movement Gandhi stated:

"This statement owes its inspiration to a personal chat with the intimates and associates of the Sabarmati Ashram . . . More especially it is due to revealing information I got in the course of conversation about a valued companion of long standing who was found reluctant to perform the full prison task, preferring his private studies to the allocated task. This is undoubtedly contrary to the rules of Satyagraha. More than the imperfection of the friend whom I love, more than ever it brought home to me my own imperfections. The friend said he had thought that I was aware of his weakness. I was blind. Blindness in a leader is unpardonable. I saw at once that I must for the time being remain the sole representative of civil resistance in action."

[6] Jayaprakash Narayan, *Why Socialism?* pp. 90–92

system. He seemed to think that this was a very desirable part of rural and national economy. This was a great surprise to me for the big Zamindaris and taluqas have very few defenders today.[7]

A further source of much irritation to the left-wing critics was Gandhi's glorification of poverty.[8] It was felt that acceptance of this principle in the circumstance of India might easily turn into a moral justification of the existing sub-human living conditions. There was a fear that acceptance of poverty would lead inevitably to the toleration, and indeed perpetuation, of the conditions responsible for poverty.

Again, Gandhi's opposition to modern science and technology caused most serious misgivings in many quarters. As early as 1909 he had declared in his *Hind Swaraj* that India's salvation lay in unlearning what she had learnt during the past fifty years:

> The railway, telegraphs, hospitals, lawyers, doctors and suchlike have to go, and the so called upper classes have to learn consciously, religiously, deliberately the simple peasant life, knowing it to be a life giving true happiness . . . Every time I get into a railway car, or use a motor bus, I know that I am doing violence to my sense of what is right. To expect to reform the world by means of highly artificial and speedy locomotion is to attempt the impossible.

Since the Mahatma never recanted his antagonism to modern science, the left wingers always had serious doubts about the feasibility of his whole programme for national reconstruction. And their scepticism was probably justifiable when one considers his remarkably unpredictable reactions to events in the world around him. His comment, for instance, on the Bihar earthquake in January 1934 was typical of a man who looked to God rather than to science for understanding. He described this terrible disaster as God's punishment for the sin of untouchability, a verdict which quite appalled Rabindranath Tagore. Nehru called it a 'staggering remark' and declared that 'anything more opposed to a scientific outlook it would be difficult to imagine'.

After the suspension of the Civil Disobedience Movement, the Mahatma, to everyone's surprise, was engaged in promoting Khaddi. As this was at a time when, to the socialists, the need for political action was more imperative than ever, his behaviour seemed quite

[7] Jawaharlal Nehru, *op. cit.*, pp. 477–78
[8] Jayaprakash Narayan, *op. cit.*, pp. 87–90

inexplicable. Many of his followers, including his closest associates, were quite unable to fathom the working of his mind. He himself admitted to Nehru that it was impossible to predict in what direction 'this unknown element in him' might lead him. Nehru has recorded his own reaction to one of Gandhi's bombshells, the Gandhi-Irwin Pact:

> I told him that this way of springing surprises upon us frightened me; there was something unknown about him which, in spite of the closest association for fourteen years, I could not understand at all, and which filled me with apprehension.[9]

This sense of bewilderment caused by Gandhi's methods obviously provided the left wing with considerable ammunition. So also did that especial bane of Indian political life, communal antagonism. The steady and deplorable growth of communalism in India had reached a decisive stage in its unhealthy progress by the early 1930's. The leadership of the Indian delegation to the First Round Table Conference had been in the hands of the Aga Khan who was regarded by the Nationalists as an arch communalist and 'reactionary'. The Aga Khan had been active in the formation of the Muslim League in 1906 and he had been its president for several years. It is hard to deny that his role as leader of the Indian delegation in London greatly stimulated communal feeling, particularly Muslim communalism.

On the other hand, it has equally to be conceded that the failure of the Congress-led Civil Disobedience Movements also encouraged the Hindu communalists. Previously over-shadowed by the Mahatma, they now dared to come out into the open. The emergence at this time led to the formation of the Nationalist Party under Lala Lajpat Rai and Pandit Madan Mohan Malaviya and to the revival of the Hindu Maha Sabha under Vir Sawarkar.

In some parts of India, notably Bengal, the communal problem was undoubtedly an expression of economic cleavages. Here the landlords were generally Hindus and their tenants Muslims, a situation which provided a fertile field in which Muslim communalists could sow unrest and sectarianism amongst the peasants. Needless to say, the communalists held highly conservative views on all social and economic questions and their tactics considerably slowed down the tempo of the nationalist movement.

[9] *Ibid.*, p. 260

The left wing of Congress was convinced that the growing communalism was both cause and effect of the failure up to now to create a mass movement for independence. Jayaprakash Narayan complained that the Congress was primarily middle class in outlook and that bourgeois ideals, ambitions and desires dominated it. Thus there had arisen a mentality which cared more for seats in legislatures than for creating a genuine mass movement.[10]

Narayan insisted that the communal problem was primarily economic in origin, and that had the Congress championed the grievances of the Muslim peasantry the growth in Muslim communalism would have been checked. The socialists therefore urged the necessity for working out universally acceptable ideals and goals which would appeal to Muslim and Hindu alike and which would thus prevent the virus of communalism from further poisoning Indian political life.

Nehru, who as his *Autobiography* reveals, was at this time increasingly disturbed by the failure of the Gandhian techniques to limit the growth of communalism, and who was increasingly attracted to socialism as a solution, was broadly in agreement with the objectives of the socialist group:

> The want of clear ideals and objectives in our struggle for freedom undoubtedly helped the spread of communalism. The masses saw no clear connection between their day to day sufferings and the fight for Swaraj. They fought well enough at times by instinct, but that was a feeble weapon which could be easily blunted or even turned aside for other purposes. There was no reason behind it, and in periods of reaction it was not difficult for the communalists to play upon this feeling and exploit it in the name of religion.[11]

The desire to limit the destructive force of communalism thus led many at this time to look to socialism as a panacea for India's social, economic and political ills. By grouping people on a class basis might it not effectively cut across those communal divisions which seemed to widen rather than contract in a capitalist India?

One of the principal weapons the socialists began to forge at this time was the youth movement. The phenomenal growth of student and youth movements all over India at this time, and their active participation in the fight for freedom, was a growing source of strength

[10] Jayaprakash Narayan, *Towards Struggle*, p. 11

[11] Jawaharlal Nehru, *op. cit.*, pp. 137–38

to the radical elements inside the Congress. The idealism of youth was being harnessed to the national struggle.

During the late 1920's and under various names, youth and student leagues had begun to proliferate all over the country. Particularly in Bengal and the Punjab, and to some extent in U.P., Bihar and Bombay, the divisions in the Congress leadership had had the effect of stimulating a keen desire for more militant action amongst the students. The founders of the Congress Socialist Party included many who had been active in the Youth Leagues like Yusuf Meherally. Anxious that the impatient youth of India should not fritter away their energies in 'adventurism', these leaders tried to divert youthful enthusiasm for rapid social and economic change into creative channels. They felt increasingly that the moderate leadership and divided mind of the Congress had little to offer Indian youth, and that since youth could be mobilised for the national movement only on the basis of a clear, radical programme, then here was favourable ground on which to sow the seeds of the socialist faith.

The left-wing group within Congress was also intent on winning over the peasants to a more militant outlook. The impact of Gandhi's mass Civil Disobedience Movements had caused a great ferment amongst the peasantry, already stirred from their traditional ways of life. Instead of looking up to the landed aristocracy as their natural leaders, the peasants had begun to pin their hopes for support and relief on the leadership of the middle classes as represented by the Congress.

There were at this time special reasons for a great surge of peasant discontent. The catastrophic fall in agricultural prices in the world depression of the 1930's created unimaginable suffering and distress in the Indian village. The economic crisis forced many peasants and small landowners to sell their land. Productivity fell and marginal land went out of cultivation; many peasants were completely ruined.

The situation of the landless labourer was even more desperate. In some places there were riots and disturbances, and a powerful impetus was given to the growth of the peasant movement all over the country. Innumerable campaigns for reduction in land rent and for the relief of indebtedness were successfully launched up and down the country. These struggles created a new sense of political awareness amongst the peasantry who as a result of coming into contact with new ideas began to question age-old assumptions.

Now the Congress attitude to this peasant ferment was never more than one of lukewarm interest. There was always the greatest reluctance to lead the peasantry against the Zamindars in Bengal, Bihar and the United Provinces, where landlordism was deeply entrenched, as opposed to the Ryotwari system elsewhere under which there was no landed middle class standing between the government and the peasants.

In this situation, the socialists felt that no opportunity should be lost of profiting from the new militancy of the peasants. National independence should be regarded not merely as a means of ending foreign rule but also as the one and only road to the emancipation of India's teeming millions of peasants and workers from exploitation and serfdom.

The determination of the left wing to bring the peasants into the nationalist movement, on the basis of a programme of agrarian reform inspired by socialist principles, was bound to lead to conflict with the landlords' interests in Congress. Acute differences arose after 1937 between the Congress Provincial Governments and the Kisan Sabha, the peasant organisation in which the Socialists were to play a leading role.

Marxism was the most important single influence in the political thinking of the younger generation of Congressmen who were now so discontented with the Gandhian techniques of struggle. They had all been profoundly impressed by the Bolshevik Revolution; news about the Russian transformation of Central Asia was now beginning to seep into India. The eulogistic accounts of the Soviet Union's First Five-Year Plan further encouraged sympathetic interest.

Though there was already some apprehension about Stalin's leadership, the Soviet experiment had become the ideal of the Indian Left by the early 1930's. Even liberals like Rabindranath Tagore were impressed by the Russians' achievements in transforming a backward economy in a rapidly short space of time. The Russians' success seemed to stand in striking contrast to the failure of the Civil Disobedience Movements, so that the radical and left-wing group within the Congress was all the more critical of the weaknesses of the Gandhian method. They became more than ever convinced of the effectiveness of the Leninist technique of struggle. It is therefore not surprising that by this time the socialists were abandoning Gandhism for Marxism-Leninism.

The question has often been asked whether there can be a place for a socialist party in a colonial situation. In other words, is it possible under foreign rule for a socialist movement to develop independently of the nationalist movement? Secondly, can a socialist society actually be established under the auspices of a foreign administration? These were two thorny problems faced by those who established the Congress Socialist Party at Patna in 1934.

From the time of its foundation, the Indian Communist Party adopted an inconsistent policy towards the nationalist movement as represented by the Congress, alternating continually between support and hostility. At this particular time the Indian Communists, under the influence of the decisions of the Sixth Congress of the Comintern, were pursuing a definite policy of opposition to the Congress. They kept aloof from the 1930 and 1932 Civil Disobedience Movements. This policy had the effect of isolating them from the national movement and caused a great decline in their influence. This example of the failure of the Communist Party to associate itself with the nationalist struggle had a profound influence on the political thinking of the founders of the Congress Socialist Party. They were convinced they would have to establish their movement and their party within the Congress itself.

It is also incontestable that a socialist movement cannot be effective in a colonial situation. There is a clash of interest between the masses on the one hand and the economic interests of the metropolitan power on the other. A colonial government, for example, can never permit the abolition of landlordism and the destruction of a capitalist economy. The whole history of colonial rule in India and elsewhere provides no convincing evidence to the contrary. This is partly because the colonial power, in order to take the fullest advantage of local resources, always has to make an alliance with indigenous vested interests. The universal pattern of the colonial system is the alliance between native feudalism and the colonial power. In every conflict that occurred in the British period between the Indian working class and the Indian bourgeoisie, the British always came down on the side of the latter, notwithstanding the fact that there was a basic conflict of interest between the Indian and British bourgeoisie, and despite the support given to the nationalist movement by Indian capitalism.

In the case of the Indian landlords, the problem for the British was even less complicated. Co-operation between the native princes and aristocracy on the one hand, and the British Government on the other, suited the interests of all parties. The British needed the Princes' support for their rule, and the feudal elements needed British protection against the peasants. This was undoubtedly the real reason for the opposition of the landed aristocracy and the Princely States to the nationalist movement.

It was considerations such as these that led India's pioneer socialists to realise that the achievement of a socialist society was impossible without first achieving national freedom. Unlike the Indian Communists, they did not make the fatal mistake of giving priority to socialism over nationalism. The right to self-determination was one of the basic tenets in the socialists' political thinking because they realised that the achievement of socialism in a colonial situation was a mirage. Unlike the Communists, they recognised that it would be fatal to go against the broad current of nationalism, and that what was really needed was not so much to press the claims of socialism against the more negative aspects of nationalism as endeavour to give a positively directed nationalism a social content.

Personalities always play a vital role in politics, and are consequently important even in a socialist movement whose leaders, as Marxists, were addicted to the most wearisome theorising about 'theses', 'lines' and 'ideology'.

The Congress Socialist Party was founded in 1934 and held its first All-India Conference at Patna in May of that year. As we have seen, socialism was 'in the air' from the time of the failure of the Civil Disobedience Movements. Socialist groups had been formed in a number of provinces by the early 1930's, being made up of those younger Congressmen who had come under the influence of either Marxism or Western democratic socialism. But the actual plan for an all-India socialist organisation seems to have been conceived and worked out at Nasik Central Prison by certain left-wing Congressmen who had been detained as a result of the Civil Disobedience Movement. The founding fathers thus became known as the 'Nasik Group'.

The most important of them was undoubtedly Jayaprakash Narayan,[12] who was destined to play a crucial role in the development

[12] For a detailed account of Jayaprakash Narayan's life see:
Ram Krishna Benipuri, *Jayaprakash* (in Hindi), Patna, 1948
Jagat S. Bright, *The Red Fugitive*, Lahore, 1946 and
Yusuf Meherally, '*Jayaprakash Narayan*' in Jayaprakash Narayan's 'Towards Struggle', Bombay, 1946, pp. 7–14

of the Party for more than twenty years. Narayan was born of middle peasant stock at a tiny Bihar village in 1903, and after attending the local English school went to the United States for university education. There he came into contact with American Communists and joined the Party. His enthusiasm for communism suffered a set-back when on his way back to India via London he discovered that the Indian Communist Party was taking its orders from Moscow. It was in accordance with policies laid down by the Sixth Comintern Congress that the Indian Communist Party was not participating in the nationalist movement.

Disillusioned by this discovery, Narayan, on his arrival back in India, joined the Congress, becoming responsible, at the request of Nehru, for the Labour Department of the All-India Congress Committee. Thus began his active political career and a personal friendship with Nehru which has been proof against all the political differences which have subsequently come between them. But though he had joined the Congress, Narayan remained a Marxist. He was especially influenced by the failure of the European Social Democratic parties to cope with the 1929–31 slump and by the growth of fascism. He thus concluded that "for a socialist party to be true to its ideals and survive it was necessary to be militant in outlook and practice".

Narayan never thought highly of the Gandhian technique of satyagraha as an effective weapon for achieving independence, and he had no faith that parliamentary democracy was likely to be any more effective. Throughout the colonial period, he was a convinced believer in the class struggle and in insurrectionary methods for achieving national as well as socialist aims. The ideas he held in this period are set out in his book, *Why Socialism?* Like many other Indian socialists, he was profoundly impressed by the achievements of the Russian Revolution and the whole technique of Soviet planning for industrialisation in a backward economy.

The westernised Narayan, who originally had little patience with Gandhian techniques, in middle age has fallen to some extent under the very spell of that traditional India which was so well symbolised in the person of Mahatma Gandhi. Narayan has now left the Praja Socialist Party to devote his life to the Bhoodan (land gift) movement led by Gandhi's disciple, Vinoba Bhave.

Another prominent Indian socialist pioneer was Yusuf Meherally. It is not easy to place him in the socialist hierarchy as he never held office in the all-India party, but his influence on its policy and programme was always very considerable. An exact contemporary of Narayan, he was born in 1903, the son of a prosperous Bombay businessman who, in accordance with family tradition, firmly supported British rule and had all the upper-class prejudices. His great-grandfather had been an industrial pioneer, building the first Indian textile mill. Meherally's imprisonment in 1930 was a great shock to his family, who described it 'as a disgrace to the family that one of its members was a law-breaker'.

As a student, Meherally studied the history of revolution and was greatly impressed by the role played in them by by organised youth movements. He read the writings of Mazzini and Garibaldi and closely studied accounts of the Russian and Chinese revolutions. Like many other Indians at this time he was deeply interested in the techniques adopted by the Irish nationalists. Meherally was an enthusiastic supporter of the first Civil Disobedience Movement and was much dismayed by its abrupt ending as well as by the unconvincing reasons given by Mahatma Gandhi for ending it. This failure convinced him more than ever of the necessity of a youth movement dedicated to the cause of national independence. His efforts led in 1928 to the founding of the Bombay Provincial Youth League which played a leading part in organising the public boycott of the Simon Commission. Following the boycott, in which he was injured in a demonstration, he achieved a prominent position in the public life of Bombay Province. From then on until his death in 1949 he was always in the thick of the political fray. It was during his second imprisonment in 1932 that he came into contact with other socialists in Nasik gaol and thus became one of the founders of the Congress Socialist Party (C.S.P.).

Achyut Patwardhan was another prisoner at Nasik who contributed to the formation of the Party, and he continued as one of its respected leaders until his retirement from politics in 1950. Born in 1905, the second son of a rich theosophist father, Patwardhan was educated at Banaras Hindu University where he was powerfully influenced by the prevailing nationalist atmosphere. After a visit to Europe, as a young University lecturer he was drawn into the Civil Disobedience Movement and ultimately found himself in Nasik Central Prison.

Patwardhan's rise in politics was meteoric. In 1936, when Nehru became Congress President for the second time, he was appointed a member of the Congress Working Committee, being the youngest man ever to achieve such high office. During the 1942 'Quit India' phase of intense agitation against Britain he played an important part in organising an 'underground' in co-operation with his socialist colleague, Dr Lohia. After 1947, despite warm personal relations with many leading Congressmen (including Sardar Patel), Patwardhan became disillusioned and in 1948 he left the Congress along with other members of the Socialist Party.

Patwardhan is a good example of the Gandhian strand in Indian Socialism as opposed to the Marxist strand represented by Narayan in his early days and by Acharya Narendra Deva. Patwardhan's Gandhism was possibly fortified by his theosophist upbringing and by the example of his elder brother, Rao Saheb. Their early influences may also have been responsible for the ultimate withdrawal of both brothers from party politics. Achyut Patwardhan now devotes himself to constructive work in the villages, being actively associated with J. Krishnamurti's movement for 'new education'.

Another member of the 'Nasik Group' was Asoka Mehta. Born in 1911 in Sholapur, he was unique in more ways than one amongst his fellow socialists in Nasik gaol. His father was an outstanding literary figure in Gujarati, and took an active interest in the promotion of education, but he died at the early age of 32. After matriculation at Sholapur, Mehta went to Bombay University where he gradually became involved in political agitation. As in the case of the others, it was the 1932 Civil Disobedience Movement that brought him to Nasik gaol.

Asoka Mehta is still a prominent leader of the Indian Praja Socialist Party. He is a good example of the social democratic strand in Indian socialism, his political thinking having been influenced by European democratic socialism. He has never been enthusiastic about the importation of Russian techniques into India and has not been appreciably influenced by Marxism. Together with Patwardhan, M. R. Masani and Lohia, he was one of the opponents of the communist inspired 'United Front'.

Mehta has a cool and logical mind which has proved both an asset and a liability for his Party. He probably excels as an organiser. His crowning achievement as a trade unionist was undoubtedly the formation in 1949 of the Hind Mazdoor Sabha. Since the First General Election of 1951 Mehta has shared the feeling of frustration and disappointment widespread in the Party, and his more recent ideas have often embarrassed his colleagues.

Other notable prisoners at Nasik who became founders of the Congress Socialist Party were M. R. Masani, S. M. Joshi and N. G. Goray. Masani, the son of a rich Parsi scholar from Bombay, studied at the London School of Economics and was influenced by Fabian thought. Like Mehta, he is a good example of the social democratic strand in Indian socialism. Masani was an important leader of the Congress Socialist Party for many years, but he later changed his ideas and turned to Gandhism. Today he is intensely anti-communist and an ardent champion of free enterprise.

S. M. Joshi and N. G. Goray have always been leading figures in the Party in Maharastra. The former is leader of the opposition in the Bombay Assembly, and the latter a member of the House of the People at the Centre. Both are prominent advocates of states reorganisation on a linguistic basis, which was till recently an important issue in Bombay.

Finally, we come to two prominent socialist leaders, Acharya Narendra Deva and Dr Ram Manohar Lohia, who were not members of the original 'Nasik Group' of socialists.

Acharya Narendra Deva, the Grey Eminence of the Indian Socialist Party until his recent death, was born in 1889. He took an interest in politics from an early age and used to attend the annual gatherings of the Indian National Congress in the company of his lawyer father. His early sympathies were with the Tilak group and he was much influenced by other revolutionaries like Lala Hardayal and Aurobindo. After the Russian Revolution, which had a profound influence on him, he immersed himself in Marxist literature to such effect as to come to be regarded as one of Marx's greatest exponents in India.

His active participation in politics began with Mrs Besant's Home Rule movement and never ceased. As he became more and more convinced of the role of the class struggle and of the importance of giving a mass basis to the Indian nationalist movement, so he began to devote himself to the organisation of the peasantry in his home province of Uttar Pradesh. By 1934 he had become one of the most important Congress leaders in U.P., and when the Congress Socialist Party was formed in that year he was asked to preside over the inaugural conference at Patna. From then onwards Acharya Narendra Deva, like Jayaprakash Narayan, was a towering figure in the Indian

Socialist Movement. His assent became the necessary *imprimatur* to any important policy decision. Unlike Narayan, he remained a Marxist, a dialectical materialist and a believer in the class struggle and the use of violence, until the very end of his life.[13]

A man of much wider cultural interests than most of his colleagues in the Party, the Acharya was essentially an intellectual. His devotion to the pursuit of social and economic justice was complete and was the outcome of a subtle and refined intellectualism. It was his total absorption in the common cause that led him to accept in 1955 at Nagpur the responsibility of leading the Praja Socialist Party at a time when its fortunes had reached a critical phase by reason of the threatened secession of the Lohia group. That the Party did not hold together in 1955 was certainly no fault of Acharya Narendra Deva. It was a consequence of the inescapable chain of events following on the breakdown of the Nehru-Narayan talks. But the Acharya's efforts to save the Socialist movement from virtual disintegration did not fail completely, and wherever today the Praja Socialist Party is an organised force, a great deal of the credit for it must be given to his outstanding courage and determination.

Finally, we come to that stormy petrel and highly controversial figure in the Indian Socialist movement, Dr Ram Manohar Lohia. Like Patwardhan, and unlike Narayan and Acharya Narendra Deva, he has not fallen under the spell of that Marxist ideology which has played such an important role in moulding the thought of the Indian Socialist movement. Lohia was born in 1910 and after attending Banaras and Calcutta Universities he subsequently went to Germany for post-graduate studies. There in the late 1920's and early 1930's he witnessed the rise of Nazism. After his return to India, Nehru put him in charge of the newly constituted Foreign Affairs Department of the All-India Congress Committee. From then until the departure of the Socialists from the Congress in 1948, Lohia played an important part in shaping the emerging foreign policy of the Congress. It was in the office of the A.I.C.C. in 1939 that he first formulated his idea of a Third Camp in international affairs at a time when the Congress was faced with the dilemma of how to support the British Government in its war effort and at the same time achieve Indian independence. From

[13] Acharya Narendra Deva, *Rastryata aur Samjawad*, Banaras, pp. 673–91
Also see Yusuf Meherally, '*Acharya Narendra Deva*', in Acharya Narendra Deva's *Socialism and National Revolution*, Bombay, 1946, pp. vii–xvi

1948 until the fatal split in the Praja Socialist Party in 1955, which he himself did so much to bring about, Lohia was principal spokesman of the Socialists on foreign affairs, and during that period he played a principal part in the formation of the Asian Socialist Conference.

As a political leader, Dr Lohia suffers from one overwhelming defect; he lacks discipline and the ability to work harmoniously with others. His extreme individualism has proved to be a crippling liability to the Socialists. Though he possesses a fresh and vigorous mind which has been responsible for many new and original activities – for instance, the formation of the Asian Socialist Conference at Rangoon – patience and perseverance have never been his strong points. He, more than any other individual leader, must be held responsible for the confusion and division that have recently reigned supreme within the Party.

We may draw two conclusions from these brief biographies of the main Socialist leaders. First, as in the case of the Congress and the Communists, the leaders of the Indian Socialist Party by social origin have tended to come from the westernised middle class. Secondly, each in his political outlook has tended to represent one of the three main ingredients that have contributed to give Indian Socialism its distinctive flavour – Marxism, Gandhism and Social Democracy. In so far as the Indian Socialist Party has had its hesitations, its crises and its failures, they can generally be traced to the difficulty of achieving a satisfying synthesis between these seemingly incompatible ingredients.

The main aim of the Indian Socialists has always been to reconcile socialism with nationalism, the two dominant forces of the age in 20th-century India. From its inception in 1934 the Party sought to prove that the achievement of national freedom and an egalitarian society were inseparable objectives. It is pertinent to conclude this paper by noting both its successes and failures in the task it set itself.

The Congress Socialist Party was what Maurice Duverger would call a party of extra-parliamentary origin. As we have seen, it arose as an expression of the profound dissatisfaction of the 'Nasik Group' of young Congressmen in the early 1930's with what they considered to be Mahatma Gandhi's unsuccessful techniques of struggle through the Civil Disobedience Movements. To the Socialists, the achievement of national freedom was only half the battle. Its real importance lay in the opportunities it would offer for the achievement of an egalitarian society, for the ideological basis of which they looked to Marx and other Western socialist thinkers. Since any progress towards such a society was out of the question in a colonial situation, they actively participated in the struggle for national freedom under the banner of the Indian National Congress. And as they were not satisfied with what they regarded as the 'go slow' policy of the Congress leaders, they campaigned from the beginning for a more militant course of action against the continuance of colonial rule. But throughout the colonial period they never lost sight of their socialist principles. From its birth the Party set itself the task of shaping and moulding Congress policy in a socialist direction. During the late 1930's the Socialists played a prominent part in building up workers' and peasants' organisations, and though they belonged to the Congress, they never hesitated to oppose it on any matter over which they felt that their socialist principles were compromised.

During the early years of its existence, the C.S.P. set itself two objectives. First, it tried to convince the Congress leaders that the successful waging of the national struggle demanded the broadening of the base of the movement by the active participation of far more workers and peasants than had hitherto been drawn in. Secondly, the C.S.P. tried to convince the masses that their struggle for better living and working conditions was intimately allied with the political struggle for freedom from colonial rule. The C.S.P. campaigned ceaselessly to get the Congress High Command to understand that the base of the movement could never be successfully broadened unless the Congress gave concrete evidence of its intention to improve the terrible social and economic conditions of the masses. That both the Congress leaders and the masses on occasion failed to realise the inseparable connection between the economic and the political struggles was certainly no fault of the Socialists. It was no mean achievement to get the Kisan Sabha and Trade Union movements to pay as much attention to the national as to the economic struggle and to get the conservative-minded Congress leaders to adopt the Faizpur Agrarian Programme.

A similar approach was adopted by the C.S.P. towards the youth movement. With the exception of the Congress itself, the C.S.P. did more than any other single group to bring the youth of the country into the nationalist fold. As on the trade union and peasant fronts, the Socialists played a major part in preventing India's youth from drifting away from the Congress through frustration over the ineffectiveness of Gandhism and other features of an essentially conservative leadership.

The Party's appeal to the Kisan Sabha, Trade Union Movement and the youth movement stemmed largely from its policy of militant action and its Marxist ideology. As we have seen, though there were undoubtedly other formative influences, Marxism was the most important single influence in the creation of the C.S.P. in 1934. Though the presence of three main strands in the Party – Marxism, Gandhism and Social Democracy – left it without ideological homogeneity, nevertheless everyone was agreed upon a radical programme for social and economic change. And here the main contribution of the Socialists to political thinking lay in their efforts to reconcile the aims and techniques of Marxism with the fight for national independence. This was where the Socialists so obviously scored over the Communists who, as the pawns of the Third International, subordinated Indian nationalism to Stalinism. The Socialists' participation in the national struggle persuaded many radical nationalists that there was no basic incompatibility between nationalism and socialism. This was undoubtedly a major achievement.

Another feature of the activities of the C.S.P. during this period was that it injected much-needed new blood into the national movement which, if not suffering from hardening of the arteries, was at least too much dominated by elderly leaders who had become set in their ideas and ways. The Socialist leaders were all young, intellectually able, possessed of immense vitality and idealism, and with the necessary strength of character and initiative to justify their claim that they could take over the leadership of the national movement should there be any faltering by the Old Guard. The importance of these qualities and the effectiveness of the Socialists as an alternative leadership could not be better illustrated than at the time of the August Movement of 1942. Only the most partisan observer would deny to the Socialists the credit for this successful display of militancy at a crucial culminating phase in the development of the national movement.

Turning to the immediate post-war phase prior to the hand-over of power, it must be admitted there was some confusion in the Socialists' political thinking. Because of their isolation during the War from the main stream of world affairs and their lack of knowledge of the momentous changes that had taken place in the general power situation, they at first failed to appreciate the radical transformation which was being brought about in the structure of the British Empire. They remained acutely suspicious of the honesty of British intentions towards India because of their doctrinaire belief that no imperialist power would capitulate unless driven by force to do so. As a consequence, their policy during the period of negotiations immediately preceding the hand-over of power was characterised by confusion and indecision.

For a time the Socialists seemed to think they were cast for a similar role to that of Mahatma Gandhi after the end of the First World War, and that they should endeavour to wrest the leadership of the national movement from the control of the 'liberal constitutionalists'. But the policy of the British Government during the years 1945–7, coupled with the Socialists' own doctrinaire approach to the problem of colonialism, led them towards a policy of hesitancy and indecision which they sought to justify by the name of 'neutrality'. By refusing either to approve or oppose the Partition the Socialists temporarily abandoned their role as the radical and militant wing of the nationalist movement and allowed the mantle of opposition to fall on the communalists, both within and without the Congress. The Party must thus share in the responsibility for the disastrous Partition.

Another but less costly error of the C.S.P. during this period was its boycott of the elections for the Constituent Assembly. It is doubtful if the Socialists could ever have exercised any really effective influence in framing the Indian constitution from within the Assembly. Nevertheless, membership of that body might have been useful as an opportunity to publicise the views of the Party on specific features of the Constitution like fundamental rights. Furthermore, the presence of two dozen or so Socialists on the opposition benches might have added something to the prestige of the Party in the country at large. And the experience gained in the actual framing of the Constitution, as well as in the debating of Bills when the Constituent Assembly sat as a legislative body, might have been useful as an initiation into the working of parliamentary government.

It took the Socialists some little time to find their feet in post-independence India. But from the outset they were careful to maintain their freedom of action by refusing to join either the Central or provincial governments. Their main problem was whether as nationalists they would be justified in actually opposing the programme and policies of India's first national government. But the general trend of Congress policies, both at the Centre and in the States, quickly led the Socialists to believe that their opposition was both desirable and justifiable. The changes in the Congress Constitution were the last straw, for they provided a clear indication that the Congress leaders were no longer willing to tolerate stringent Socialist criticism from within their own ranks. Thus excluded from power within the Congress, the Socialists took their historic decision at the Nasik Conference in 1948 to break away from the Congress.

The decision to part company with the parent organisation was both a 'pilgrimage into the wilderness' and an 'adventure into utopia', and we are bound to ask ourselves whether this momentous step was really necessary. Such a question takes us to the heart of the Socialists' political thinking. To the founders of the C.S.P. the real meaning of Swaraj had always been not simply the ending of colonial rule but the emancipation of the masses from exploitation and injustice. Since the initial performance of the Congress Governments held out little hope of a radical social and economic programme, and since its policies were clearly intended to serve the interests of the Indian capitalists and landlords, the Socialists were, according to their own lights, perfectly justified in breaking away. By doing so, they not only remained true to their political principles, but they also gave a lead to those who were rapidly losing faith in Congress promises.

The Socialists' separation from the Congress served another purpose. Although India after independence had chosen a parliamentary system of government, it was difficult to see how it could take root without a parliamentary opposition willing to play this most difficult political game according to the recognised rules. Not only was the Congress a monolithic party, but such opposition to it as existed came mainly from the Communists and other revolutionary groups who were hostile to the whole concept of parliamentary democracy. But by 1948 the Socialist leaders were becoming increasingly convinced of the feasibility of achieving socialism in India by evolutionary rather than by revolutionary methods. The main influences on their political thinking had come from their new contacts with Western social democrat leaders and their increasing knowledge of life behind the Iron Curtain countries. The Indian Socialists had always been convinced that political democracy was incomplete without economic democracy. Their study of one-party rule in the Soviet Union and other communist countries now convinced them that economic democracy (if even that existed in Russia) was incomplete without political democracy.[14] The more they studied the institutional aspects of

[14] *Policy Statement of the Socialist Party*, Bombay, 1951, pp. 6–7

socialism in the communist countries the more appalled they became at the lack of political freedom. This led them gradually to a realisation of the value of such Western achievements as a free press, free trade unions and opposition parties dedicated to the overthrow by peaceful means of governments in power.

Thus the general result of the break-away from the Congress was to accustom the Socialists more and more to the idea that they should constitute the core of a radical but responsible opposition within the framework of parliamentary government. Their entry into the political arena as an independent party with a militant social and economic programme, but wedded to parliamentary democracy, thus offered an alternative to those who had become disillusioned with the Congress, but who had no wish to turn to the Communists. It was considerations such as these that won the Party much of its support in its main strongholds of Bombay, Bihar, U.P., Assam and Madhya Pradesh.

Nevertheless, it would be idle to pretend that the Socialists broke away from the Congress simply because they were suddenly obsessed by a mission to stand forth as the only radical but responsible opposition parliamentary party. This could scarcely be proved, as some of the Socialist leaders have remained to this day unconvinced about the applicability of Western parliamentary democracy, without modifications, to Indian conditions. This brings us to what, to any Western observer, must seem the most baffling feature of Indian Socialism – its attempted synthesis of the seemingly contradictory elements of Marxism, Gandhism and Social Democracy.

Although some of the leaders might be pointed to as exceptions, it would be true to say that the general outlook of the Congress Socialist Party from 1934 to 1947 was that of doctrinaire Marxism. It was based on hostility to Gandhism and to parliamentary government in the restricted form in which the British permitted it to function in colonial India. The principal danger of the Socialists' Marxism during the period from 1934 to 1942 was that it might lead to their capture by the Communists, the fate which overtook so many European Socialist parties. Not only did a founding father of the Congress Socialist Party like Narayan start his political life as a Communist, but in the late 1930's there was every incentive to form a 'united front' with the Communists against imperialism and fascism. The parting of the ways undoubtedly came in 1942 with the "unpatriotic" action of the Communists in supporting the British war effort in India. Ever since then the intense nationalism of the Indian Socialists has led them to keep the Communists at arms' length.

Since independence, Gandhian Socialism and Western Democratic Socialism have been incorporated, along with their original Marxism, into the political thinking of the Socialists. The former antagonists of the Mahatma have now taken over certain aspects of his teaching like *satyagraha*, inseparability of ends and means, and decentralisation both in government and industry, all of which they feel can be successfully used under Indian conditions for the achievement of a socialist society. Jayaprakash Narayan, under the influence of Vinoba Bhave, and in the Indian tradition of renunciation, has even created his own *ashram* in Bihar in pursuit of 'constructive work' in the villages. At the same time the Socialists have come more and more to recognise the importance of the liberal tradition in Western Democratic Socialism, especially in its emphasis on the rights of the individual.

Indian Socialism, by virtue of the element of Gandhian Socialism, is thus far from being the wholly foreign importation it once seemed likely to be in the days of the leaders' largely unmodified Marxism. But though the recent Gandhian element in the Socialists' social, economic and political thinking, to a non-Indian, may seem the most surprising of the three constituents – particularly in view of the C.S.P.'s antagonism to the Mahatma in the colonial period – to an Indian Socialist today it is possibly the most natural. The spell of the Mahatma binds in varying degrees not only the Socialists but all political parties in India except the Communists.

Can one say that a satisfactory synthesis has been achieved? No one looking at the history of the leaders' differences of opinion and their frantic theorising could make any such claim. A synthesis may be emerging, but it has not yet been achieved. The major incongruities between these three strange bedfellows are still clear for all to see. Marxism postulates violence as the basis of the state; Gandhism postulates non-violence. Marxism puts the emphasis on centralised planning and industrialisation; Gandhism is rooted in anti-industrialism and decentralisation of both government and industry. Marxism and Gandhism are opposed to parliamentary government; Social Democracy can use no other instrument. To reconcile such incongruities the Socialists have come out in favour of decentralised planning, and *satyagraha* as an alternative to parliamentary action. But decentralised planning to a Western Socialist may seem a contradiction in terms and resort to *satyagraha* is quite incompatible with the recognised procedures of parliamentary government. Nevertheless, despite the obvious inconsistencies, it may well be that the three main elements will ultimately achieve a fusion in the minds of the Indian Socialists. That the task is not inherently impossible is evident from the psychology of Nehru himself, which is a compound of Marxism, Social Democracy, Western liberal ideas and Gandhism.

It must be conceded however that ideological differences within the Party, combined with the anarchical attitude to discipline evinced by such leaders as Lohia, have undoubtedly deprived the Socialists of the much-needed cohesion which was vital if the Party was to become an effective political force. The lamentable performance of the Socialist leaders after the First General Election is a case in point. Even more amazing was the subsequent retirement of most of the top leaders of the Party from active politics.[15] Such an abdication of responsibility by leaders of a party which still wished to win votes at elections is almost without a parallel. In this sense, the Socialists have been their own worst enemies. They started with enough disadvantages, even if they had been united in outlook. They had little or no funds with which to make headway against a political machine like the Congress, which had the backing of both landlords and industrialists and a high degree of cohesion and discipline brought about by years of struggle as a national movement. But largely through their lack of political realism and their inability to do their arguing amongst themselves behind closed doors like any other disciplined party, the Socialists succeeded in weakening their Party by their publicly advertised internal schisms far more than it was ever weakened by its opponents' criticisms. But for the disastrous dissensions which emasculated the Party after 1952 it might have fared far better than it did at the Second General Election in 1957. At that time, and as the results show, there was much dissatisfaction with the Congress, and the Socialists' idealism and integrity should have been major political assets in their favour.

It might of course be argued that the extra-parliamentary origin of the Party played some part in depriving it of political realism and in fostering political indiscipline. The Congress had had the invaluable experience of both fighting previous elections (though it is true they were on a restricted franchise) and in running the Provincial Governments

[15] These leaders were Jayaprakash Narayan, Kamaladevi Chattopadhyaya, Ramandan Mishra

after 1937. In the process, it had thrown up astute party managers and political bosses like Sardar Patel, who were adepts at hushing up dissension with a firm and resolute hand. The Communists, in addition to ample funds and a highly efficient political organisation, had even more ruthless methods of purging the sharp critics within their own ranks. But the Socialists fell between two stools. They had neither the parliamentary experience of the Congress nor the ruthlessness of the Communists. Though their leaders' decisions, only too often, were imposed on an acquiescing rank and file, the leaders insisted on the democratic right of thrashing out their differences in public. The results were disastrous.

Yet it would be wrong to end on a note of pessimism. Despite their failure in the field of organisation, the Socialists have made their own unique contribution to Indian politics. It is their role as 'unofficial policy makers' that will probably be seized upon by future historians as their particular claim to fame. The Socialists have included in their ranks some of the most intelligent, nimble and discerning minds of modern India. They have been intensely articulate and very clear-sighted. For years they have acted as a continual goad spurring on the unwieldy, slow-moving conservative Congress in the direction of a socialist India. After all, it was largely Socialist pressures which brought about the Congress agrarian programme in the 1930's. It was the Socialists, and not Mr Nehru, who first advocated neutralism as the foreign policy most appropriate for free India. And it would not be going too far to say that Congress 'Socialism' itself, as expressed in the Avadi resolution, arose largely out of the pressures for social and economic reconstruction exerted by the Socialists.[16] These are achievements which may be remembered long after the Party's shortcomings as a political organisation have been forgotten.

[16] See: *A Programme for National Revival*, Bombay, 1950, and *Thirteen Point Programme of the Hind Kisan Panchayat to End Poverty*, Bombay, 1950

# THE PROBLEM OF INDIAN IMMIGRATION TO CEYLON

*By Nimalasiri Silva*

OF THE VARIOUS issues facing any modern government in Ceylon, "the Indian problem" constitutes one of the major premises on which political issues are formulated. We may trace the history of the Indian problem in Ceylon back to the 1820's with the introduction of the cash-crop plantations into Ceylon. At that time the population of Ceylon was approximately two and a half million. When large-scale plantations were begun it was not possible to obtain local labour in sufficient numbers to work these big estates. The Ceylon peasant saw no reason to accept an employment which restricted his way of life without greater economic benefits. However, as the coffee plantations of the Central highlands were opened by British capital and management, the planters solved the problem of labour by importing "large quantities of cheap labour" [1] from South India.

In order to put this Indo-Ceylon problem, as it is known today, in its proper perspective, it is important to recognise certain features which characterise its development from the middle of the last century. First of all, after over three generations of association with Ceylon the migrant Indian population has not been absorbed into the indigenous population. These South Indian wage-earners who live on the Kandyan plantations still observe the social traditions of South India. They are different in religion, language, social traditions and occupation from the Sinhalese population in the Kandyan villages. They did not at any time form part of the traditional village community life which existed in the valleys below the tea plantations. Thus one finds today the Kandyans in the valleys, cultivating their ancestral lands, while on the hillsides a separate community of Indian labourers exists observing the social traditions of South India.

Many such families in Ceylon maintain contact with their relatives

[1] *Labour Conditions in Ceylon, Mauritius and Malaya.* Report by Major G. St. J. Orde Browne, Cmd. 6423, 1943

in India and visit their ancestral villages every year. Even families which have been long resident in Ceylon maintain contact with India, so that, for instance, the young men marry wives from within the appropriate social groups in India. The population is migrant also in the sense that it is not attached to the soil but moves about from estate to estate as employment offers.

Within the same province, the same district and even the same village area there are thus two distinct communities, unable to speak each other's language, having no social or economic relations with each other, and having in fact nothing in common save geographical propinquity. This is the picture so far as the Indian population resident on the estates is concerned. This population constitutes by far the largest proportion of the Indian population in Ceylon.

Indians thus form both the largest group of immigrants into Ceylon and the largest group of aliens resident in Ceylon. If one considers the distribution of population in Ceylon according to race, there are 974,098 Indian Tamils resident in Ceylon. A further 47,462 Indian Moors resident in Ceylon must be added to this figure. These are the figures of the last general Census in 1953. In terms of the increase in population during the past few years from 1953 to 1957 of 2·5% per annum which brings the total population of Ceylon to 9,237,506 persons, there ought to be a proportionate increase in the Indian residents, subject of course to the fluctuations of migrations.

But outside the estate areas, and more especially in the towns, there is a not inconsiderable section of Indians who are just as migrant and who are by profession hotel-keepers, barbers, domestic servants, moneylenders, and business men, and whose presence is no less significant to economic conditions in Ceylon.

*Nature and Growth of the Conflict*

The political aspect of "the Indian problem" arose when the Royal Commission of 1927 appointed to report on Constitutional Reform in Ceylon recommended universal adult franchise for Ceylon in respect of the entire population. The Commissioners recommended that a qualification of five years' residence in the Island (allowing for temporary absence not exceeding eight months in all during the five-year period) should be introduced in order that the privilege of voting should be confined to those who have an "abiding interest" in the country or who may be regarded as "permanently settled" in the

Island. They described this condition as "of particular importance in its application to the Indian immigrant population".[2]

When in 1929 the Donoughmore Report was debated in the Ceylon Legislative Council, the principle of abiding interest and permanent settlement as a condition of the franchise met with general acceptance, but the method of its application caused acute controversy.

The Sinhalese leaders felt that the five-year residence test of the Donoughmore Commissioners would enable the Indians to swamp the Sinhalese vote in the Kandyan areas. They feared the consequences of the unrestricted extension of the franchise to the Indians, for it would have virtually enfranchised the entire Indian estate population.

Accordingly the Sinhalese leaders demanded that the five-year test of past residence formulated by the Donoughmore Commissioners should be reinforced by a further indication of intention to remain in Ceylon and become a permanent part of the island's population.

To meet this demand it was proposed that domicile (which quite simply defined means: *A person's regular and legal place of abode*) either of choice or origin, should be made the standard test of citizenship.[3]

It was also proposed that for domiciled and undomiciled alike the preliminary requirement of "British nationality and a minimum age qualification of 21 years" – was essential.[4] Under this system practically all Ceylonese and quite an appreciable number of Indians would have been entitled to registration as citizens of Ceylon.

For the undomiciled – and this in fact meant the large majority of the *migrant* Indian workers resident on the plantations – two further conditions were added in order to obtain a clearer indication of intention to remain in Ceylon:

(*a*) A declaration of intention to settle permanently in the Island.
(*b*) A renunciation of any claim to special rights, privileges or protection by any Government other than the Government of Ceylon.

The satisfaction of these conditions entitled an applicant to a Certificate of Permanent Settlement granted by a specially appointed officer and was regarded as proof of citizenship.

[2] Report of the Royal Commission on Constitutional Reform in Ceylon (1928), Cmd. 3131, p. 81

[3] Sir Herbert Stanley (Governor of Ceylon), Sessional Paper 34 of 1929, p. 13

[4] Cmd. 43668, p. 56, para. 205

It was on this understanding that the Legislative Council, by a majority of 19 to 17 votes, accepted the Donoughmore Constitution of 1931. On the other hand, this modification of the Donoughmore Commission's recommendation excited considerable apprehension in India and an official protest was made to Whitehall by the Government of India. H.M. Government, however, replied that this did not constitute a substantial modification of the constitutional proposals and that they did not seem "to involve any racial discrimination against, whereas some of the Indian protests amounted in effect to a claim to a position of privilege rather than of equality".[5]

As a result of these changes (as embodied in the operation of Ceylon State Council Elections-Order-in-Council of 1931) the number of Indians registered as electors in that year was about 100,000 as compared with the 12,438 registered in the Indian electorate under the old constitution – an increase of over 700%. In the first semi-responsible State Council under the new Constitution the Indian electorate sent in 7 members out of a Council of 54, one of whom became Minister of Industries.

Succeeding years, however, have not stifled the controversy over this matter. On the one hand, the Sinhalese maintained that the administration of the Elections Order-in-Council had been contrary to its spirit and intention. On the other hand, the representatives of the Indian community in Ceylon complained of administrative efforts made to reduce the Indian voting strength.

The Soulbury Commissioners, reporting in 1946 on the working of the existing Election-Order-in-Council, stated that the Sinhalese complaint "seemed to rest on surer foundations". Between 1931 and 1936, the period of the first State Council, the number of Indians registered had risen to 145,000 and by the beginning of the second World War, out of a total population of about 670,000 Indian estate workers and their dependents, more than 225,000 were registered as voters.[6]

In 1938 representations were made by the Sinhalese[7] to the Governor, Sir Andrew Caldecott, that the regulations governing the Indian franchise had not been properly implemented. In his famous Reforms Despatch of the same year, the Governor stated that it was "not a

[5] Lord Passfield (Secretary of State for the Colonies), Seessional Paper 34 of 1929, p. 24

[6] N. K. Sarkar, *The Demography of Ceylon* (Government Press, Colombo, 1957)

[7] Sinhala Maha Sabha Deputation, March 1938

question of constitutional reform but of tightening up the procedure and as such would receive his careful attention".[8]

As a consequence of this, in 1940, the procedure on the *revision of registers* was altered in regard to the qualification of domicile of choice, and instructions were given that no facts relating to the question of domicile were to be accepted unless they had been *checked* by a Registering Officer or an Enumerator, and no one was to be registered who was not *orally* examined. Thus from 1940 onwards the figures of registration of these Indians declined and the number in 1943 (four years before the elections to the first Parliament of Ceylon) amounted to about 168,000.

This aroused all the old fears of discrimination in the minds of Indians. They maintained that "the complexity and uncertainty of the domicile test when exerted so rigidly on a mass of illiterate people cannot be a positive obstacle to the legitimate enfranchisement of many Indians".[9] The spokesmen of the Ceylon Indian Congress were stronger and more militant in their protests. Feelings were beginning to harden on both sides.

The Soulbury report points out, however, that this "tightening-up" process stemmed from a remarkable feature of the registrations since 1931 – that practically all those who appeared for examination and were successful in establishing their claim to registration obtained their qualification in respect of domicile – mainly domicile of choice – and only a few hundreds in respect of the Certificate of Permanent Settlement.[10] Considering that this Certificate was devised in order to overcome the difficulties and complexities attendant upon application for registration in respect of domicile, it was remarkable that the Indian estate workers made so little use of it. Thus proving that a considerable number of Indians were admitted to the franchise under an Article which, if correctly and strictly interpreted, would have made their admission difficult.

One reason was perhaps their fear that by applying for and obtaining the Certificate the applicants would relinquish their right to any protection which they might otherwise expect from the Indian Government. This attitude prompted Sir Baron Jayatilleka to say in the Ceylon State Council, "it epitomises the mentality of Indian labour in general,

[8] Sessional Paper 28 of 1938

[9] Annual Report of the Indian (Government) Agent in Ceylon (1944)

[10] Report on Constitutional Reform in Ceylon (1945), Cmd. 43668, p. 59

they have one foot in the plantations of Ceylon and they wish to have the other planted firmly in India".[11]

"The fact, however, remains", states the 1946 Special Commission Report, " that since 1940, in spite of the tightening-up procedure, substantial numbers of Indians acquired the franchise in virtue of domicile." The Report estimates that at least 80% of the Indians whose names appeared in the Preliminary Lists were either born in Ceylon or had resided in Ceylon for at least ten years.

That was the political and constitutional position of the Indian worker under the sixteen years of the Donoughmore Constitution from 1931 to 1947. Under the laws of this period the Indians controlled a good 15% of the Legislature, and by means of the Executive Committee system of the State Council, which enjoyed full responsible government in all internal affairs, a great deal of social and industrial legislation was passed which affected the welfare of the worker.

Acts such as the minimum wages (Indian Labour) Ordinance 1935, Estate Wages Board Act 1936, Maternity Benefits Ordinance of 1939 were important landmarks in the history of social welfare affecting all workers irrespective of race, caste or creed.

The same period saw the rise of an organised Indian trade-union movement. The Ceylon Indian Congress gradually became a most vociferous and well-organised champion of the Indian worker, and the estate management had to take increasing cognisance of the Party Agent in the matter of estate labour-relations.

*The Problem as Dealt with in the Soulbury Constitution*

With the appointment on the 5th June 1944 of the Special Commission to formulate proposals for Constitutional Reform in Ceylon, the status and rights of Indians were once again brought into the forefront of national politics. Ceylon Indians agitated for a detailed Bill of Fundamental Rights with special reference to the franchise restrictions. The impending transfer of political power to the Ceylonese caused racial and communal feelings to be roused up again. The fears of the minority communities of possible domination by the Sinhalese released a strong agitation for communal forms of representation. The demand of the communal All-Ceylon Tamil Congress for a 'fifty-fifty' form of representation in a Parliament of 100 members between the majority and minority communities embraced the Ceylon Indians too, and

[11] *Hansard*, Proceedings, Ceylon State Council, March 1944

far from easing tensions, only tended to make the Indians more feared as they were now being associated with a larger political movement of Tamils, including possibly those of South India. The Soulbury Commissioners, after having gone into the question of Franchise and Representation thoroughly, left the basis of suffrage in Ceylon untouched. Thus, as under the Donoughmore Constitution, Ceylon domicile was made the standard test for the franchise. The system of enfranchising Indians remained the same.

On the general principle that any country possessing full responsible government in all internal civil administration has the right to determine the future composition of her population, the Soulbury Contribution maintained "that the United Kingdom Government could not interfere with any restrictions the Ceylon Government may make upon the entry of aliens".[12]

The Soulbury Commissioners took, however, due care to ensure certain fundamental safeguards for the minority communities. It embodied into the new Constitution (by Article 29) the fundamental principle that no person of any racial or religious community could be made liable to any disabilities or restrictions to which persons of other communities or religions are not made liable. By six nominated seats in a House of Representatives (Lower House) and by a process of nomination and election to the Senate, minority interests were further strengthened and safeguarded.

*The Economic Aspect*

The conflict between the immigrant Indians and the Ceylonese in the economic sphere did not flare up until the end of the first World War when the national sentiment of the Ceylonese advanced rapidly and was demanding self-expression in every field. The feelings of the Sinhalese towards Indian immigrants was expressed as follows:

> There can be no doubt that unduly large numbers of Indians are coming to Ceylon every year in search of employment. If the present influx continues, this country will soon have more immigrant labourers than are necessary for its requirements (if indeed the limit has not already been reached) and it will have to face the problem of their repatriation, this country will soon be swamped by Indian immigrants.[13]

[12] Cmd. 43668, p. 63

[13] D. S. Senanayake, Presidential Address: Ceylon National Congress, 1926

With the spread of English education, the educated youth amongst the Ceylonese found the more lucrative avenues of employment more or less blocked, the only employment open to them being the few subordinate and clerical posts in the Government departments. Almost all the non-European posts in the commercial firms were largely monopolised by the educated Indian immigrants. In the field of business and trade they found the Indian traders, experienced and with vast resources, well-established rivals against whom they had little chance. Naturally, their bitterness against the alien rose higher with every frustration that they met.

The decade between the mid-thirties and the end of the war only emphasised both the political and economic aspects of the problem. By 1946 the total population had risen to over six million and was increasing rapidly. The pressure of population in the rural sector led to an inadequacy of land and to fragmentation on the one hand, and to a willingness on the part of the Ceylon peasant to seek employment in the estates on the other. He saw that whilst there was under-employment in the peasant sector, there was regular employment in the estate-sector. While all the adults in an Indian estate family could obtain employment, thus achieving comparative prosperity, the sole bread-winner in a peasant family was not even sure of employment or of an adequate income. It is therefore understandable that the up-country peasant saw in the Indian Tamil an active economic enemy.

The economic depression and the great malaria epidemic which hit Ceylon in the 1930's brought into even greater focus the economic aspect of "the Indian problem". The main difficulty was that the population had been increasing steadily since the beginning of this century, whilst the expansion of the economy had almost stopped some twenty years earlier, so that the economic resources were increasingly strained. The depression of 1930–6 dealt a severe blow to the plantation economy of Ceylon and the middle-classes of Ceylon, along with all other classes, faced economic ruin. The small landowners were often completely ruined; even the owners of large estates had to mortgage their properties. The Indian moneylenders – the Chettiars – seized the opportunity to gain control of as much land as possible, so much so that a Land Redemption Ordinance had to be passed to alleviate the condition of the now-impoverished upper middle-class.

The labour market, skilled and unskilled, was flooded with Indian immigrants who left the estates for Colombo and other towns in search of employment. A crisis was impending when the great malaria epidemic broke out in 1935 amongst an undernourished population, irrespective of nationality and race, taking toll of 80,000 lives.

The presence of a large Indian population in Ceylon thus came to be regarded as a restriction of employment opportunities for the Ceylonese. A special Committee was appointed in February 1939 to investigate the problem, and in November of the same year the Board of Ministers set about applying a policy of Ceylonisation which excluded Indians from Government employment, except in special circumstances, and later of stopping unrestricted immigration into Ceylon.

While the increase of their numbers was sharpening the conflict between the Ceylonese middle and labouring classes and the Indians, a different attitude was developing amongst the wealthier classes in Ceylon. As Ceylonese capitalists began to replace the European planters they too became interested in maintaining the flow of cheap Indian labour.

Meanwhile the Indians had formed a strong organisation to safeguard their interests – the Ceylon Indian Congress. It claimed a close association with the Indian National Congress, and used its prestige among Indian estate workers to gain their support. It succeeded in organising the estate labourers into a single strong trade union. For the first time the planters, European and native, were faced with organised labour.

The leaders of the Ceylon Indian Congress, mostly merchants themselves, were opposed to the separation of the question of the estate workers from that of other Indians. They realised that Indian estate workers were necessary to the Ceylonese planters and that the Ceylonese would be especially glad to get rid of the Indian merchants and moneylenders. Hence their effort to associate the interests of the other Indian groups with those of estate labourers.

*The Post-Independence Era*

In order that discussions over the franchise might not delay the attainment of independence, the first elections under the Constitution of 1946 were held on the 1931 franchise, but power was given to the new Parliament to regulate the matter and decide on its own citizenship laws. The elections showed how close the communal ties were among the Indians.

The Kandyans were virtually disfranchised in seven up-country constituencies where the Indians were in a majority owing to the geographical contiguity of the plantation areas. Where they were not in a majority the Ceylon Indian Congress vote went almost solidly in support of the leftist candidate thus swinging the whole election against the majority elements who were conservative in character but divided in substance.[14]

It is believed that in 14 constituencies the Ceylon Indian Congress secured by these means the election of a candidate who had only minority support among the Ceylonese voters. Thus a communal organisation exclusively representing the Indians affected the result in one-fifth of the total constituencies in Ceylon.

This encouraged closer contacts between Ceylon Indian Congressmen and Indian political leaders, particularly in Dravidian South India, so much that it began to exacerbate relations between the Ceylonese and Indian communities and threw fresh doubts regarding the genuineness of their "abiding interest in Ceylon".

With the attainment of Independence by Ceylon in Febraury 1948 the Senanayake Government addressed itself to defining Ceylon citizenship. The Prime Minister himself said:

"As I have stated before, the change in our status makes it necessary, if this country is to be an independent country, that the people of this country and the people of this country alone, should have the right to determine who their legislators should be." [15]

This was the prevailing mood and it characterised the attitude of the ruling United National Party Government towards Indo-Ceylon relations.

The Government maintained that the principle underlying the law of franchise was that a person who can exercise the franchise must be a citizen of that country. "Persons whoever they may be who claim this country alone as their motherland and who intend to stay here and work for this country will have the right to vote without any other consideration." [16]

Prospects of a satisfactory settlement of the Indo-Ceylon impasse seemed very bright when the Prime Ministers of India and Ceylon reached "broad agreement" in December 1947 at New Delhi on the

[14] I. D. S. Weerawardena, *Ceylon University Review*, February 1947
[15] *Hansard*, Ceylon House of Representatives, July 13th 1948
[16] *Hansard*, J. R. Jayawardena, House of Representatives, November 29th 1948

special conditions qualifying Indians already resident in Ceylon for Ceylon citizenship. The agreed formula was as follows:

(*a*) A period of continuous residence for seven years for persons who are married and ten years for unmarried persons, preceding 31 December 1941, provided that such period of residence shall have been completed prior to 31 December 1945. Absence exceeding one year shall constitute a break of continuous residence.

(*b*) Adequate means of livelihood.

(*c*) If married, the wife and minor unmarried children if any should have ordinarily have resided with the applicant.

(*d*) He should be in a position to comply with the laws and customs of the country and

(*e*) No Indian who is admitted to Ceylon citizenship would be allowed to retain Indian citizenship.

When this formula came to be implemented important disagreements arose between the Government of Ceylon and the Government of India. There were two points of disagreement. First, the Ceylon Government maintained that only those who continuously resided in the period immediately prior to the Appointed Date qualified for citizenship. The Government of India, on the other hand, maintained that as long as an applicant had put in the necessary residence any time previous to the Appointed Date and not necessarily immediately before it, he had qualified for citizenship.

But the Government of Ceylon was not willing to accept this interpretation of the formula. This was the major point of disagreement. Secondly, the Ceylon Government maintained that the residence qualification should be accompanied by the further test of adequate means of livelihood. That is, that those who qualified for residence, but had no means of livelihood, should not be given citizenship. The Government of India, on the other hand, maintained that no unemployed person should be disqualified on grounds of inadequate means of livelihood but only the unemployable. However, the Ceylon Government went on to implement these proposals which were embodied in the Indian and Pakistan Residents Citizenship Act of November 1948.

The Prime Minister of India further maintained that Ceylon Citizenship as envisaged by the Ceylon Government drew a sharp distinction between citizenship by descent and citizenship by registration, discriminating against registered citizens who were thus relegated to an inferior status. He asked for an assurance from the Ceylon Government that there will be no discrimination, either legislative or administrative, between citizens by descent and citizens by registration. Mr D. S. Senanayake in his reply dated 19 August 1948 stated that he could give the required assurance (they agreed on a number of points such as jointly taking action against illicit immigration and the preparation of a separate electoral register in Ceylon of all those registered under the Act) only in respect of eligibility for franchisement or for public office, but that his Government did not propose to remove any legal restrictions in Ordinances such as the Land Development Ordinance, the Fisheries Ordinance, and the Omnibus Licensing Ordinance which may operate against certain classes of citizens by registration.

The negotiations therefore reached a stalemate. Meanwhile, the Ceylon Indian Congress called for a boycott of the so-called "inferior" citizenship offered and applications for registration by resident Indians as citizens were few. The Ceylon Indians' criticism against the qualifications prescribed for citizenship was that they were prohibitively rigorous and the procedure too cumbersome and that a means-test for the majority of Indian labour with its chronic indebtedness was difficult of fulfilment. The Ceylon Indian Congress, however, lifted the boycott after seven out of the twenty-four months prescribed for citizenship: "it decided to give the Act a trial".[17] There was a rush of applicants for citizenship.

In January 1954 the stalemate was temporarily ended when Pandit Nehru and Sir John Kotelawela, the then Prime Minister of Ceylon, met at New Delhi and arrived at a "substantial measure of agreement". They agreed on a number of points such as jointly taking action against illicit immigration, the preparations of a separate electoral register in Ceylon for all those registered under this Act. The October talks, however, spotlighted a new and fundamental difference that had arisen between the two Governments, but left it unsettled. Ceylon recognised no "stateless" Indians, and India would now recognise as her own only Indians who held Indian passports and Indians who had obtained Indian nationality under the Terms of Article 16 of the Indian Constitution.

It was however agreed that the two processes of citizenship registra-

[17] Annual Report of Ceylon Indian Congress, 1949

tion would be speeded up, so that the position might be reviewed at the end of two years. Ceylon said she would encourage registration as Indian citizens by permitting persons so registered to remain undisturbed in their employment until the age of 55, and she reiterated that she had in mind a scheme of financial inducements too. India once again undertook to give every opportunity and every facility to Indians to register themselves as Indian citizens. The significance of the 1954 Pact lay in the fact that it was the first major instance where both sides had made fair concessions.

The number of persons who have been registered up to the end of 1958 is 101,199, about one-tenth of the total Indian population.

The Ceylon Indian problem, then, is presently crystallised in three correlated enactments:

1. The Ceylon (Parliamentary Elections) Amendment Act No. 48 of 1949, which by limiting voting rights only to those on the last certified electoral lists of 1950 virtually excluded the entire Indian estate population from the franchise because it was largely a shifting one.
2. The Indian and Pakistan Residents (Citizenship) Act, which to some extent liberalised the opportunities for persons of Indian and Pakistan origin with an "abiding interest in the Country" to acquire Ceylon citizenship.
3. The Ceylon Immigration and Emigration Act of 1949, which was a logical corollary to the definition of Ceylon citizenship and which governed the movements of non-nationals to and from Ceylon.

## AUTHORS OF PAPERS

RAGHAVAN IYER is Agatha Harrison Memorial Fellow and Lecturer at St Antony's College, Oxford. He formerly worked in the Indian Planning Commission.

GUY WINT is a Leverhulme Research Fellow attached to St Antony's College. He is the author of *The British in Asia*, *Spotlight on Asia*, and *Dragon and Sickle*, and co-author of *India and Democracy* and *Middle East Crisis*.

KYRIL TIDMARSH is on the staff of the International Labour Office, Geneva. He did research at Nuffield College on Russian political thought in the nineteenth century. His paper was written in 1957 when he was a Fellow of St Antony's College.

HARI KISHORE SINGH is a Lecturer in Political Science at the University of Banaras. He was previously at St Antony's College, doing research on the Socialist Party of India.

NIMALASIRI SILVA is in the Foreign Service of Ceylon. He recently spent a year at Queen Elizabeth House, Oxford.

ST. ANTONY'S PAPERS NO. 8
South Asian affairs I.